THE NATIONAL AND TATE GALLERIES

THE NATIONAL AND TATE GALLERIES

By R. N. D. WILSON

WITH ONE HUNDRED
PLATES IN COLOUR

THOMAS NELSON AND SONS Ltd.
LONDON EDINBURGH PARIS MELBOURNE
TORONTO AND NEW YORK

TO

LOUEY C. JACK

A LOVER OF THE ARTS

IN

GRATITUDE AND AFFECTION

LIST OF PLATES IN COLOUR

LIST OF PLATES IN COLOUR

LIST OF PLATES IN COLOUR

NOTE

THE British National Gallery of Pictures was founded in 1824 by the purchase by the State, at the suggestion of King George IV., of thirty-eight paintings from the Angerstein collection. These were exhibited for some time at Mr. Angerstein's house in Pall Mall. The building in Trafalgar Square, designed by William Wilkins, was opened to the public in 1838.

The Tate Gallery was founded in 1897 as a Gallery of Modern British Art. The Turner Wing was added in 1910.

In 1915 the Trustees of the National Gallery, with a view to making the collection at the Tate a National Gallery of British Art in the fullest sense, recommended that paintings of the British School should be transferred there from Trafalgar Square, and that only a comparatively small number of selected masterpieces, sufficient to represent the British School on the same footing as those of other countries, should be retained at the National Gallery.

This was carried out in 1919, when more than two hundred paintings of the older British School were transferred to the Tate Gallery from Trafalgar Square. The collection remaining at Trafalgar Square was strengthened by the addition of certain outstanding works by British painters of the nineteenth century, brought from Millbank.

The fine galleries for Modern Foreign Art at the Tate Gallery were opened in 1926.

The official title of that Gallery is now the National Gallery, Millbank, though it is still popularly known as the Tate Gallery.

INTRODUCTION

I

FAMILIARITY can blunt the edge of our impressions. How many of those who pass through the turnstiles of the National Gallery ever stop to consider how immense is that transition? Outside swirls one of the nerve-centres of our highly-mechanized civilization. The confusion of its sights and sounds seems scarcely to have receded when we find ourselves face to face with the glow of early Italian altar pieces, painted by men who lived in a world vastly different from ours, more different in its sense of spiritual values and general trend of thought than it was in actual appearance, though the archaic remoteness of the latter is immediately striking. The contrast is so marked that for many it is apt to be a little confusing. I have watched people drifting past those hieratic masterpieces, perplexed by their primitive and childish conventions, looking for something and prepared to be impressed, for the very sound of the phrase " Old Masters " carries with it a sort of title-deed to admiration. I have even been rude enough to listen-in to some of their comments, as when an elderly and indefatigable lady, pausing before the Della Francesca " Nativity," remarked to her slightly younger companion, " My dear, what terribly plain-looking faces." I gave her full marks for candour, always a welcome and refreshing commodity. The truth is, there is a great deal to be said for the I Know What I Like approach to painting.

But it is not enough. Most of us would like to find a reason for our preferences, something that will relate the pleasure we derive from Manet, with our reactions to Mantegna, and explain why Filippino Lippi moves us, while Landseer leaves us cold. This analysis of experience, interesting as it is for its own sake, has a further use. It can sharpen our appreciation and increase our capacity for enjoyment. That is the chief thing. Art exists to quicken us with a delight, a mental and emotional excitement completely distinct in kind—I am convinced—from that which any other objects or contacts whatsoever can afford. Any theory of æsthetics that is not founded upon this basic experience is valueless.

A picture is primarily an appeal to the senses, and through them to the imaginative reason. Before we approach it sufficiently close to study its representational content we are aware of certain things,

INTRODUCTION

the pattern produced by the arrangement of its masses and colours, the rhythm of its design, the key of tonality in which it is pitched. These things are a stimulus in themselves ; they are the mediums which the painter uses to convey his emotion. The subject is of secondary importance. Any subject that awakes a creative response in the artist is sufficient. A still-life by Cézanne, a kitchen chair painted by Van Gogh, because they are informed by the intensity of the painter's vision, excite us ; while an elaborate historical composition by Alma Tadema, carefully arranged and executed with a photographic fidelity, leaves us quite unmoved. It is not the subject that matters ; it is the transmutation that it undergoes.

It follows that not every painting is a work of art. That is not to say that such paintings may not perform eminently useful functions. They can be documents of great human interest. Frith's " Derby Day," for example, is a pageant of English life in the eighteen-fifties. It is painted extremely well, and can give us a vast amount of pleasure and information, but our reactions to it are of a completely different order to those which we experience from a work of art. I do not pretend that the distinction may not often be a difficult one to make. There are numerous border-line cases. But a work of art is something which evokes in us a particular emotion, call it the æsthetic emotion, if you will, and this has its genesis in the artist's intensity of feeling communicated to us by his handling of visual form. His problem is to convey that original emotion intact, without letting it become dissipated or diffused. To do this he has to build up an internal harmony of forms, summoning to his aid balance and rhythm and pattern, all the subtle relationships of line and colour that give force to and modify each other by juxtaposition, as words do in poetry. These are qualities which exist in the mind. They have not an independent existence in nature. Art is not an imitation of nature. It is the imposition of the artist's perception upon what he sees.

So much for generalities. How are they to be applied ? What relationship do they bear to the early Italian religious painters who are our first consideration ? Surely they were out to convey ideas, to inspire devotion, to present what to them were dogmatic truths. I agree. But I hasten to add that our participation, or non-participation (as it is more likely to be), in their beliefs has nothing whatsoever to do with our response to their paintings. An intelligent Buddhist can derive as much from them as the most orthodox Christian. It is true that they painted religious subjects, and Christianity, with its emphasis upon the Word made flesh, provided them with an objectivity peculiar to its anthropomorphic genius. The theme of the Madonna and Child, of the Nativity, of the agonizing tragedy of the Cross (and how few representations of the Crucifixion are even remotely painful) afforded an infinitude of stimulus, capable of direct translation into visual reality. It is only in so far as such concepts had been *seen* that they are pertinent to art. And they were seen with a consuming intensity by those early artists. Had they been mere pietists or moralizers or purveyors of abstract ideals, such as Watts, their work might well have been negligible. It is their obvious delight in the handling of line and colour with a simplicity and purity which has seldom been equalled that constitutes their appeal to all ages.

Their technical resources were limited; the conventions of perspective were only being discovered; the device of chiaroscuro was unknown to them; but those very restrictions gave them a certain advantage. They were not tempted into the byways of facile representationalism. Primitive art is always arresting by its directness. So little mechanism comes between the original concept and its translation into form.

We are so accustomed to paintings which exhibit the artist's skill in his imitation of nature, that possess a power of stimulus by their handling of perspective and naturalistic lighting effects, that to many the work of the Primitives may appear somewhat crude. They will be disappointed at not finding certain qualities which they expect in a picture. To such I would suggest: Do not begin with Primitives. Study those masters that make an immediate appeal to you, and gradually, as your perception of form in painting increases, you will be able to appreciate the Primitives as well.

II

MR. SINCLAIR LEWIS in one of his novels of life in the Middle West describes a lecturer who in the course of a single talk, given to one of those circles of enthusiastic if rather undiscriminating ladies that seem to flourish in the States, professed to deal with English literature from Chaucer to Browning. I cannot hope to compete with that compacton. Fortunately in this book the pictures are the thing; they do the talking. But a few generalizations, that may summarize the salient features of the various schools represented, may be of service in enabling us to take a bird's-eye view.

The Italian masters come first in time as they do in importance. They enunciated and laid down the principles that are at the root of all European painting. Their art derived from two sources, that of the Byzantine workers in mosaic, and of the Græco-Roman fresco painters of classical times. The Byzantines taught them the value of pure and magnificently glowing colour, and of simplified design. The Græco-Roman artists contributed a realistic note, secular and close to mundane actuality.

Giotto (1266–1337) may be considered the father of Italian painting.

Unfortunately he is not represented in the Gallery. In him the two traditions met and blended to produce something entirely new to art. He had the spiritual intensity and sense of design of the Primitives, but his figures are not merely transcendental and hieratic personages, they are creatures of flesh and blood. So great was his achievement that after him his immediate followers seem to be marking time.

Then the Florentines, Uccello by his study of perspective, Masaccio and Piero della Francesca through their solution of the problem of rendering three dimensional volume in painting, the Pollaiuoli by their researches into anatomy, enormously increased the artist's scope. The full Renaissance dawned, and giants like Michelangelo and Leonardo da Vinci summed up in themselves a plenitude of being and power of creation that have never been surpassed. Michelangelo was a sculptor, and that fact is felt throughout all his painting. It is rash to generalize, but on the whole it may be said that the genius of Italian art inclined to the sculpturesque. The discipline of sculpture, with its concentration upon the essentials of mass, of the equipoise of movement, in its discarding of detail, or rather in its subjection of such to a unity of design and composition, possesses invaluable advantages. It might well be part of the training of any artist.

After Florence, Venice gathered to itself the greatness of Italian painting. Colour, I suppose, is the distinguishing mark of Venetian art. Titian added the stimulus of tactile values to the resources previously exploited. He painted texture as well as volume. The Venetian love of magnificence, of pageantry, is seen in the work of great decorative artists such as Tintoretto and Veronese. Something spiritual was lost. The purely sensuous element in painting was increased. But to the end, to the lovely swan-song of Tiepolo, they preserved their sense of design.

It is easy to see the glamour that Italian art has always possessed for painters of other lands. Yet it has its dangers. It has led many to the imitation of conventions not fundamentally native to their own genius. It has resulted in the production of a vast number of works couched in the rhetorical style known as the " Grand Manner." A poet may have a profound admiration for Milton, but he cannot afford to imitate him without sacrificing his own personality. Art, if it is to be vital, must always be in direct relationship to its own age.

III

WITH the Schools of the Netherlands we enter another world. Again it is risky to generalize, but Sir Charles Holmes suggests that the ideal the Netherlandish painters had before them was that of the open window. He dwells upon the effect of the long northern winters, and of the comparative smallness of the rooms in Flemish and Dutch town houses. His remarks apply particularly to the Dutch cabinet pictures and landscapes, but they are suggestive in reference to the work of these lowland artists as a whole. " A painted piece of blue sky or vivid sunshine, so vivid as for the moment to seem almost real, would be a comfortable possession on a gloomy afternoon, as would one of those conversation pieces which enable us to peep, as it were, through the picture frame into another room and find good company there."

It is an interesting fact that the earliest Flemish painting we have illustrated, Van Eyck's " Jan Arnolfini," contains a circular mirror reflecting the room in miniature, and painted with a vast amount of skill and minute observation. That intimate realism is a recurring note in all Flemish and Dutch painting. From the outset it was more concerned with representationalism than was Italian art.

The early religious paintings were a development of the work of the monkish illuminators and miniature painters. They retained many of their qualities. The method of painting in glazes of transparent oil colours, brought to perfection by the Van Eycks, enabled the Flemish artists to give a high surface finish to their pictures, and to indulge in a microscopic elaboration of details. But there is something stilted about Flemish religious art. It is precious rather than abounding. A series of annotations rather than a moving epic.

Rubens came as a liberator. He brought movement and the excitement of sweeping design into later Flemish art. He brought a fluency of colour, an exuberance of brushwork, that supplanted the hard enamel-like technique of the earlier painters. His pupil Van Dyck carried this resiliency to England, and passed it on to Gainsborough, whose sensitive touch added to it a refinement that made it in his hands the vehicle of the most exquisite painting our country has ever seen.

The Dutch masters are exceptionally well represented in the National Gallery. On the whole we can consider the majority of them as being fundamentally realistic. The average Dutchman was a matter-of-fact person. He was not speculative in the sense that the Italians, notably the Florentines, were. He had taste, and he was "house-proud," if one may use that term in an extended significance, to include his attachment to his family, to the well-being that rewarded his industry, to the security of his social institutions, to his unostentatious religion, and to his country, now his own on the termination of the long and bitter struggle with the Catholic powers.

Dutch art was essentially domestic. Pictures were regarded as articles of furniture, intimate household gods. Portraiture was an adornment of the family tree. The cabinet pictures and landscapes mirrored the life the artist saw around him ; they are tributes, as it were, to the *genius loci*, to the deities that presided over the pursuits of the hearth, the conviviality of the tavern, and pleasures of the countryside. Hence it is only to be expected that Dutch painting should exhibit a realistic turn of mind. Its representational qualities are so importunate that they tend to come between one and that purely æsthetic intensity which is the real end of art. Sometimes in the handling of light, as in the case of Vermeer (PLATE 61), as in De Hooch's " Interior of a Dutch House " (PLATE 59), we are moved by the miracle. The transmutation that we demand has been effected. The painter's vision is translated into terms of light, brilliant, vibrant, intoxicating, and the result stirs us, as does an Italian master's handling of volume and movement. But the range of such invention is essentially a limited one. In Dutch painting, with few exceptions, it is confined to paintings of interiors.

There remains Rembrandt. He is singularly detached from his contemporaries. His work is informed by a depth of human feeling possibly unique in the annals of art. For that reason one's reactions to him are of a complicated nature. I find him a difficult master to fit into any preconceived theory of æsthetics. For my own part, I must confess that the keenest pleasure I derive from him is one that is not predominantly æsthetic. Much of his work does not move me at all. When I am stirred it is nearly always by some note of purely human emotion, of pity or of love. A work of art can inspire such feelings, but they seem to me to be incidental, of secondary importance, to its appeal to the absolute æsthetic sense as such. Michelangelo's " Entombment " (PLATE 16), for example, does not arouse in me any profound sorrow. I am immediately so excited by his superb handling of plastic forms that I forget everything else. With Rembrandt my reactions are reversed. The human impact comes first. Then I am aware that it has been conveyed to me by an extreme sensitivity of touch and an amazing economy of means, especially in the use of colour. To say this may indeed be the highest form of praise. There is something (though not everything) of truth in the dictum—*Ars est celare artem.* Rembrandt was a psychologist as well as an artist. He was so interested in character, in the drama, and, above all, the poignancy of human relationships, that he subjects everything to their expression. It drove him to explore all the effects that can be produced by the conflict of light and darkness, by contrasts in the force or delicacy of his brushwork. Sometimes his hand seems to tremble in a gentle hesitancy, sometimes it loads the canvas with crumbling masses of paint. Under such an impetus a less masterly technique might well have broken down. At times he seems to be striving to convey emotions that lie beyond the gamut of painting, that require the intonation of the spoken word, the living gesture of the stage. That is possibly why I find it so difficult to analyse my response to him. He disturbs so many of my preconceptions that one ends by confessing " Others abide our question, thou art free."

INTRODUCTION

IV

It is impossible to generalize about the Spanish School as a whole. Art did not develop in Spain with the same continuity that is to be observed in countries like Italy or the Netherlands. It would be truer to say that it broke out sporadically.

For the purposes of a summary survey such as this, we could do worse than confine our attention to three remarkable masters, El Greco, Velazquez, and Goya. They have an importance, not only for their own sake, but because they have had a considerable influence on the trend of modern painting.

El Greco (1545–1614), or to give him his real name, Domenico Theotocopoulos, was not a Spaniard by birth; he hails from Crete. Of Hellenic descent, he was known as " The Greek " in the land of his adoption. At an early age he went to Venice, where we hear of him as a pupil of Titian's. In 1575, being then about thirty, he came to Spain, and settled in Toledo, where he lived and worked until his death. The sources of his art are difficult to assess. We can detect a Byzantine influence. That of Titian would seem to be conspicuous by its absence. Of the Venetians, Tintoretto and Bassano left a certain imprint, but of a truth his was a strikingly original genius that formed its own conventions. He was of a religious temper, and the fervour of Spanish Catholicism was more congenial to him than the comparative laxity of Venice. Many may find a hint of fanaticism, of hysteria even, in the violence of his concepts. Certainly they were of a kind more likely to meet with acceptance in Spain than in any other country.

The National Gallery is fortunate in possessing two fine pictures from his hand: " Christ driving the Traders from the Temple " (1,457), and " The Agony in the Garden " (3,476). Movement was the medium that he found most expressive of his vision. For it he was ready to sacrifice representational accuracy, and throw to the winds the rules of conventional proportion. He preserves the sense of volume, for mass increases the momentum of his figures. His forms are flamelike in their intensity. They leap and writhe as though possessed by some inward impelling force. His colours flicker and flash with the violence of lightning. He saw things as in that apocalyptic hour when " the veil of the temple was rent in twain from the top to the bottom, and the earth did quake and the rocks rent ; and the graves were opened, and many bodies of the saints which slept arose, and came out of their graves and went into the holy city, and appeared to many."

But it is useless to try to describe the effects he creates. They must be seen to be credible. So intense was his apprehension of form, so electric his handling of it, that he remains one of the greatest

INTRODUCTION

exponents of the creed of pure æsthetics that Europe has ever known.

Velazquez was of a different temperament, less violent, much more human. Both he and El Greco have had a profound effect on modern art, El Greco by his passionate sense of form, Velazquez by his use of colour. The subtlety of Velazquez' handling of paint, the intimacy of his response to actuality, were qualities that were to engage the attention of Manet and subsequent painters. He is represented by two famous works in our illustrations, so we can pass on to Goya, the last of the trio.

Francisco José de Goya y Lucientes (1746–1828) was an eccentric genius. His life was as exciting as his art. He was of a turbulent disposition, continually getting into scrapes. There is a fierce satirical touch about much of his work. It can be seen in " The Bewitched " (1,472), an illustration of a scene from a play by Zamora. A priest frightened by demons, who appear to him in the forms of animals, is pouring oil into a lamp held by a goat. It is full of horror and mystery, conveyed to us by Goya's magical handling of blacks and greys. His two portraits in the National Gallery are vivid and arresting. The freedom of his technique (at times the vivacity of his touch recalls the subtlety of Velazquez or the dazzling improvisations of Tiepolo), combined with his violent fantasy, his feeling for the macabre, his delight in the picaresque, produce a result that is incommunicable in words. His art is one of the bridges between the eighteenth century and the modern age.

V

THE British School has been dealt with at considerable length in the text. I propose to devote my remarks here for the purpose of repairing certain omissions.

Hogarth can be regarded as the father of modern English painting. His " Shrimp Girl " (PLATE 66) strikes a note that is typical of English art at its best, a freshness of outlook, a spontaneity of handling, a happy naturalism, which, when they have been pursued by our native artists, have led them to their most memorable successes.

The eighteenth century saw the rise of our classical school of portrait painters. On the whole their importance has been over-estimated. It gave us, it is true, the genius of Gainsborough. Increasingly we are becoming aware of his greatness, " all that sweetness in such strength." What Purcell is to English music, he is to our painting. Both had certain airs and graces, an elegance belonging to their age, but both have left us something that the change of prevailing fashions cannot affect, a radiant purity, a lyrical quality, a sheer loveliness, that is as fresh to-day as it was then.

INTRODUCTION

England's greatest contribution to art, however, lay in the direction of landscape painting. The work of Constable and Turner is exceptionally well illustrated in this volume, so there is no need to anticipate here what has been said in the text. It is a misfortune that the aims of such painters as Hogarth, as Constable, and Cotman were overlooked to a great extent during the first half of the nineteenth century. English painting descended to mere anecdotalism. William Blake (1757–1827) was too eccentric a genius to pass on his fiery impetus. And at any rate his work, impressive as it is, trespasses beyond the bounds of legitimate art. But a visitor to the Tate Gallery must stop in the Blake Room to study his powers of visionary design, and to admire the beautiful mosaic pavement made by Mr. Boris Anrep.

The pre-Raphaelites did their best to rescue English painting from the mediocrity in which it was floundering, but they gave it a false orientation. The association of art and literature is always a dangerous one, and it has been particularly so in this country. Painting must always stand on its own feet. It loses in force when it attempts to become a handmaid to poetry.

Yet the pre-Raphaelites produced some interesting pictures. Sir J. E. Millais (1829–1896) left in his " Christ in the House of His Parents " (No. 3,584 in the Tate Gallery), and in his " Ophelia " (No. 1,506 in the National Gallery), two works that have an arresting quality. The latter especially is remarkable. Its profusion of detail is subordinated to the effect as a whole. The vivid emerald green which is the predominating colour note is used with a certain emotional emphasis. But art of this kind is a hothouse plant, nurtured in an artificial atmosphere. From the beginning to the end there was something vitiating about the pre-Raphaelite approach to painting.

Ford Madox Brown (1821–1893), whose " Christ washing Peter's Feet " has been transferred to Trafalgar Square, achieves in that work a definite power of expression. But the influence of the pre-Raphaelites proved his undoing. " The Last of England " (No. 3,064 in the Tate Gallery) has a certain human interest, a mid-Victorian quaintness, but little artistic merit.

Holman Hunt (1827–1910) seems to me to have been just incredibly bad. Burne-Jones (1833–1898) is dealt with (I hope not too unkindly) in the text.

No survey of Victorian painting would be complete without a mention of G. F. Watts (1817–1904). To many he will be associated with the figure of a blindfolded lady sitting on a globe, and nursing to her bosom a musical instrument that must surely be one of the strangest ever devised. (It has always seemed to me to consist of a broken chair-back to which had been wound a spindle of thread.) She is, optimistically enough, called " Hope." This work shows to what a pass the desire to purvey ethical ideals, to preach sermons in paint, can bring a really good artist. For Watts had the makings of an artist in no small measure. He had a grasp of decorative design, and considerable powers as a colourist. "For He had Great Possessions" (No. 1,632 in the Tate Gallery) shows him at his best. There he was painting something that could be translated into terms of actuality without recourse to such stage-properties as broken lyres and the music of the spheres. We are moved by the severe sweeping simplicity of his design. The allegorical concept is of secondary importance. Watts had qualities that English art could ill have spared, but they were led into directions outside that of legitimate painting. He remains a warning, as much as anything else.

The salvation of English art in the closing years of the nineteenth century came from France. The achievement of French painting during that century had been as remarkable as was the absence of distinction, for the most part, on our side of the Channel.

The founding of the New English Art Club in 1886 marked the recognition of the new principles of reality. Painters realized that the quest of poetic imagery, of abstract metaphysical ideas, or, as an alternative, of dull academic representationalism, was as of nothing in comparison to that vivid apprehension of nature, an emotional contact with actual visible reality. As a result fresh life came into English art, a vitality that is still producing exciting works.

The phenomenon of Whistler (1834–1903) demands a separate notice. He lies a little outside the main stream of development. He had exquisite taste, a wonderful subtlety of tonal values. He was quick to see in the conventions of Japanese art a means of achieving that refinement of expression which he sought. He succeeded in composing pictures all highly articulate in their " arrangement " (it was his own word), all extremely personal in their idiom, that move us with a kind of fragile beauty, the lethe of a deliberate monotone. Time has not impaired their static loveliness, but it has revealed a certain lack of vitality. No one would dream of attacking him to-day on the grounds that Ruskin did. He had immense skill, but the self-imposed limitations of his style ended by becoming a mannerism. When such happens something essential is lost.

With Whistler may be mentioned Sargent (1856–1925). He had an innate sense of style, but his success as a portrait painter led to his failure as a creative artist. He dazzles us by his amazing facility, by his cleverness, but he repeats himself so often that we begin to wonder whether he has anything to say. One questions whether the honour of an entire room at the Tate Gallery devoted to his portraiture may not have been rather an exacting form of tribute. It is an ordeal only the greatest could survive.

Thanks to the progressive spirit of those directing the policy of the Millbank Gallery, the work of contemporary English painters can be studied at the Tate. Sickert and John are well represented, so is Wilson-Steer. Stanley Spencer's mysterious " Resurrection " will not pass unnoticed. Henry Lamb's " Phantasy," with its vague reminiscence of Picasso, excites me. So does the work of Paul and John Nash, of Vanessa Bell, of Alvaro Guevara. Bernard Meninsky's " Portrait of a Boy " is surely one of the most beautiful of recent acquisitions. On no account should it be missed.

But it is invidious to mention names. Any one with eyes in his head can see that we need have no reason to despair of the state of art in our midst. If there is a lack of any unanimity of aim, if the variety of individualistic points of view and of technical methods is bewildering, that is all to the good. It is one of the conditions of life.

VI

THE French School is not represented at the National Gallery with the fullness it deserves. Neither is it in this book. The six examples, which make such a beautiful conclusion to our illustrations, are taken from the Tate Gallery, and are representative only of the modern French School. It is impossible by mere description to hope to fill in the gaps. Readers who can visit the National Collections will be able to surmount these difficulties for themselves.

French painting does not by any means begin with Poussin (1594–1665). But he is the earliest French master really adequately represented at Trafalgar Square. He has obviously been influenced by his study of Italian art, and is one of those rare northern painters who have been able to profit by an Italian schooling. There is a quality of logic about his work, a power of handling dramatic movement, an architectural solidity of form, that entitle him to his place as one of the immortals. He has been described as the father of " heroic landscape," and in the work of Claude Lorrain (1600–1682) we can see how this aspect of his art was to germinate. Claude's " Marriage Festival of Isaac and Rebecca " (No. 12 in the National Gallery) is a piece of pure landscape painting, serene and transparent in its loveliness. Turner would be the first to acknowledge his debt to him.

The Wallace Collection is richer than the National Gallery in French work of the eighteenth century, but since it is outside our province we can pass on to the beginnings of nineteenth century art in France.

The modern school may be said to date from Corot (1796–1875) and Courbet (1819–1877). Corot in a sense is the more important, for the modern spirit manifested itself first in landscape. The change was a subtle one. It is easy to describe it as a return to nature, but it was more than that, it was to nature seen with a vivid personal vision. Corot in his later style could make a clump of willows by a pool the text, as it were, of a lyric in paint, the embodiment of an emotion existing in his mind, evoked indeed by nature, but bending nature to its will. " The Palace of the Popes, Avignon " (No. 3,237 in the Tate Gallery), belongs to his earlier period, when he was still under the influence of the classical tradition. It is tranquil and spacious. The folds of the landscape, broken by the pale escarpment of the palace, are set before us with a wonderful feeling of expanse. The colouring is simple in its restraint. Afterwards he was to attempt more atmospheric colour effects, which paved the way for, though they did not actually anticipate, the Impressionist movement. But many will prefer the definition of his early period to the misty harmonies of those romantic improvisations by which he is chiefly known.

Courbet was of a different calibre. He remained a realist, and his " Interment at Ornans " (in the Louvre) is a superb, if rather sombre, *tour de force*. He is not represented by any outstanding work in the Tate Gallery.

Corot's influence made itself felt on the painters of the Barbizon School. Our own Constable played a part in the new development. The exhibition of his " Hay Wain " (PLATE 79) at the Salon of 1824 excited much admiration by reason of its open-air freshness. The Barbizon painters issued no doctrinaire manifesto. They were united by a bond of sympathy, an instinctive response to nature, the expression of which differed according to their varying personalities. Millet was one of them. His studies of peasant life are world famous. His draughtsmanship was better than his colour, and he did not entirely avoid the pitfalls of sentimentality, but he has a sincerity that is moving. Work such as his would have been inconceivable in the eighteenth century.

The increasing pursuit of atmospheric effects, above all of naturalistic lighting, led to many experiments. It was an age of great artistic activity, and a feeling of discovery was in the air. The revolution came when a group of remarkable artists, of whom Monet, Manet, Renoir, Sisley, and Pissarro were the leaders, united themselves under the banner of Impressionism. Technically their point of departure lay in the painting of light. They discovered that light was made up of primary colours. They discarded the dull hues, the heavy opacity of shade, and used a palette of high quivering tones, unbelievably new in their brightness. The innovation they made effected the most sweeping changes. It is no exaggeration to say that it is the one original development in modern art. It led to a totally new range of colour expression.

Pissarro (1830–1903) was one of the profoundest Impressionists. He is represented by three fine works at the Tate Gallery—" Printemps, Louveciennes " (3,265), " Côte des Bœufs " (4,197), and " Le Boulevard des Italiens : Effet de Nuit " (4,119).

Claude Monet (1840–1926) had not Pissarro's depth. His charm lies less in the searching quality of his vision than in the magical iridescence of his atmospheric effects. How wonderful these are can be seen from his "Le Bassin aux Nymphéas" (4,240), a study of a lake in the artist's garden at Giverny. It is an incredibly beautiful tissue of colour and light.

Renoir (1841–1919) had an equally remarkable feeling for colour, which he carried into the realm of figure painting. "La Première Sortie" (3,859), a picture of a young girl in a box at a theatre, is a singularly good example of his art. His pictures exhale colour. They are enveloped in a sort of chromatic musk, sometimes almost oppressive, like the scent of tuberoses.

Manet (1832–1883) was a different person. His relationship to the Impressionist movement is dealt with in the text and need not be discussed here.

We have said enough to introduce the reader to the group of French pictures with which this book closes. It would be difficult to overestimate the importance of those painters. Their work has leavened the whole of modern art. It will continue to do so, not only on account of its as yet unexhausted technical possibilities, but because it has reasserted the supremely important truth that art has its roots in the depth of the artist's perception, in his passionate reaction to life, and that where such is lacking, no amount of merely imitative skill can atone for the defect.

BIOGRAPHICAL INDEX

BELLINI, Giovanni (1428 ?–1516), one of the founders of the Venetian school; son of Jacopo, and brother of Gentile Bellini; painted religious subjects, also portraits; master of Titian, Giorgione, Palma Vecchio, Lorenzo Lotto, and others. PLATES 22, 25.

BOLTRAFFIO, Giovanni Antonio (1467–1516), School of Milan; follower of Leonardo da Vinci; noted for his portraits. PLATE 20.

BOTTICELLI, Sandro (1444–1510), Florentine School; known by his nickname which means " Little Barrel," derived from a sign which hung outside his brother's shop in Florence; real name was Alessandro di Mariano di Vanni dei Filipepi; apprenticed at fifteen to a goldsmith, entered the studio of Fra Lippo Lippi; one of the circle of artists at the court of Lorenzo the Magnificent; in 1482 summoned to Rome by Pope Sixtus IV. to paint frescoes in the Sistine Chapel; fell under the spell of Savonarola in his later years, and abandoned painting; died in comparative poverty in 1510. PLATES 9, 10, 11.

BOUTS, Dirk (1400–1475), Flemish School; born at Haarlem; settled at Louvain in 1440; painted religious subjects and portraits. PLATE 39.

BURNE-JONES, Sir Edward, Bart. (1833–1898), English School; educated at Oxford, met William Morris and D. G. Rossetti, and decided to become a painter; worked with them in decorating the Oxford Union; designed cartoons for stained glass and tapestries; his work suffers from a spurious " mediævalism." Died at Fulham. PLATE 89.

CAMPIN, Robert (1375–1444), Flemish School; influenced by the Van Eycks. A vigorous painter who had for pupils Roger van der Weyden and Dirk Bouts. PLATE 38.

CÉZANNE, Paul (1839–1906), French School; landscape, still-life, and portrait painter; born at Aix en Provence; went to Paris, 1861, where he met Pissarro; studied in the Louvre; first sent to the Salon, 1866; his work was rejected then and thereafter, but has been one of the strongest influences on modern art. *Vide* Clive Bell's *Art* and *Since Cézanne* (Chatto and Windus). Settled in Aix, and died there. PLATE 97.

CLAUSEN, Sir George (1852–1944), English School; influenced by Bastien Lepage; devoted himself to painting impressions of rural life and the study of sunlight direct from nature. R.A. 1908. PLATE 90.

CONSTABLE, John (1776–1837), English School; born at East Bergholt, Suffolk, where his father was a well-to-do miller. A great landscape painter, one of the few English artists who have had an influence on the Continent. Died at Hampstead, and buried in the parish churchyard there. PLATES 78, 79, 80, 81.

CORREGGIO, Antonio Allegri da (1494–1534), School of Parma; born at Correggio, near Modena, son of a cloth merchant; painted religious subjects, but cannot be considered to have had a religious cast of mind; famous for his flesh painting, and one of the earliest artists to use oil paint in the modern manner. Died at the age of forty in his native town. PLATE 19.

COSIMO, Piero di (1462–1521), Florentine School; pupil of Cosimo Rosselli, from whom he takes his name; noted for his interpretations of pagan mythology; master of Andrea del Sarto. PLATE 14.

CRIVELLI, Carlo (1430–1493), Venetian School; worked at Ascoli, in the Marches of Ancona; used tempera in preference to oils, and delighted in profuse ornamentation. Well represented in the National Gallery, which possesses eight of his works. PLATE 23.

CROME, John (1768–1821), English landscape painter; born Norwich; known as Old Crome to distinguish him from his son, also an artist; founder of the Norwich School; painted without affectation and with a feeling for atmospheric effect. PLATE 77.

CUYP, Aelbert (1620–1691), Dutch School; born at Dordrecht; noted for his pastoral scenes. In addition to those at Trafalgar Square, the Dulwich College Gallery contains sixteen of his works. PLATE 57.

DAVID, Gerard (1464–1523), Flemish School; born at Oudewater, in Holland; settled at Bruges in 1483; painted religious subjects with an honest gravity. PLATE 42.

DEGAS, Hilaire-Germain-Edgar (1834–1917), French School; painter, pastellist, and lithographer; born in Paris of rich parents; Salon 1866 exhibited the first of his series of pictures of horse races; Salon 1868 the first of his famous studies of Ballet Dancers; had a vivid and sensitive touch, and chose his subjects from contemporary life. Died in Paris. PLATE 96.

DYCK, Sir Anthony van (1599–1641), late Flemish School; portrait painter; born at Antwerp; pupil of Rubens; invited to England by Charles I., who appointed him court painter; knighted 1632. Died in London and was buried in Old St. Paul's. His remains perished in the Great Fire of London a quarter of a century later. PLATE 49.

EYCK, Jan van (1390–1441), early Flemish School. Along with his elder brother Hubert (b. 1366?) founded the School of the Netherlands. In 1425 became official painter to Philip "The Good," Duke of Burgundy; resided at Bruges, but travelled extensively; made important technical discoveries in the use of oils; famous for the minuteness of his finish, and acute powers of observation. PLATES 36, 37.

FRANCESCA, Piero della (1415?–1492), Florentine School; born at Borgo San Sepolcro; executed famous series of frescoes at Arrezzo; studied perspective, and is noted for the sculpturesque solidity of his figures; worked with the Florentine artists of his day, but returned to Borgo San Sepolcro, where he died and is buried. PLATE 3.

FRANCIA, Francesco (1450–1517), School of Bologna; born there; trained as a goldsmith, and became Master of the Mint; an eclectic painter of religious subjects, considerably influenced by Perugino. Died at Bologna, where his entire life had been passed. PLATE 8.

GAINSBOROUGH, Thomas (1727–1788), English School; born at Sudbury, Suffolk, married and settled at Ipswich; removed to Bath in 1760, where he met with recognition. In 1774 came to London, where he maintained a rivalry with Sir Joshua Reynolds as a portrait painter. Greatest of the eighteenth-century English portraiturists. An original member of R.A., but ceased to exhibit in 1783. Died in London. PLATES 70, 71, 76.

GAUGUIN, Paul (1848–1903), French School; born Paris; went to sea, then entered a bank; began painting in 1871, pupil of Pissarro and friend of Van Gogh; went to Tahiti, 1891, where he found the environment best suited to his genius; famous for his studies of native life, and for his powers as a colourist. Died at Dominique (Antilles). PLATE 99.

GHIRLANDAIO, Domenico (1449–1494), Florentine School; apprenticed to a goldsmith who was noted for his jewelled garlands, "ghirlande," hence his surname; painted frescoes, notably those in Santa Maria Novella, Florence; had as pupil Michelangelo. Died of the plague in 1494. PLATE 12.

GOGH, Vincent Van (1853–1890), Dutch School; painter of still-life, landscape, and portraits; born at Zundert; after trying various vocations took up painting only seven years before his tragic end; friend of Gauguin; possessed a remarkable intensity and directness of style. PLATE 100.

GUARDI, Francesco (1712–1793), Venetian School; pupil of Canaletto; painted views of Venice. In addition to those at the National Gallery, the Wallace Collection possesses nine of his works. PLATE 35.

HALS, Frans (1580–1666), Dutch School; born at Antwerp, but spent most of his life at Haarlem. Famous for his portraits, the best of which are full of vitality. Improvident by nature, he ended his days in poverty. Died at Haarlem. PLATE 50.

HOBBEMA, Meindert (1638–1709), Dutch School; born at Amsterdam; landscape painter; friend of Ruisdael, by whom he was considerably influenced; earned his livelihood as a Customs official. PLATE 63.

HOGARTH, William (1697–1764), English School; born in London; started as an engraver, and continued to issue engravings up to his death. After 1728 turned to oil painting, studying under the painter Thornhill, whose daughter he married. Famous as a satirist, e.g. his series "The Harlot's Progress" (1731), "The Rake's Progress" (1735), and "Marriage à la Mode" (1745). Admirable portraiturist, fresh and striking in his style. Not unjustly regarded as the father of the modern British School. PLATE 66.

HOLBEIN, Hans, the Younger (1497–1543), German School; son of Hans Holbein the Elder; engaged in portraiture, mural decoration, and the production of woodcuts, including the celebrated "Dance of Death" series; court painter to Henry VIII., 1532. PLATE 44.

HOOCH, Pieter de (1629–1677?), Dutch School; born at Rotterdam, but lived mostly at Leyden and Delft; painter of conversation pieces famous for their exquisite finish and handling of light. PLATES 59, 60.

JOHN, Augustus Edwin (1878–), English School; born at Tenby, Wales. R.A. 1928; renowned as portrait painter; has also painted still-life and landscape, and executed mural decorations; one of the greatest of living artists. PLATE 93.

KONINCK, Philips de (1619–1688), Dutch School; born at Amsterdam; landscape painter, pupil of Rembrandt. PLATE 56.

BIOGRAPHICAL INDEX

LIPPI, Fra Filippo (1406–1469), Florentine School; son of a butcher, brought up by Carmelite monks; romantic and wayward, he quitted the cloister in 1431; fell in love with a young nun, Lucrezia Buti, whom he abducted from her convent. In 1457 she became the mother of Filippino Lippi. Pope Pius II. absolved the pair from their vows. Fra Lippo Lippi died at Spoleto after a short and sudden illness. His paintings are informed by a warm humanism. PLATE 5.

LIPPI, Filippino (1457–1504), Florentine School; son of Fra Lippo Lippi and Lucrezia Buti; entered the studio of Botticelli; completed the frescoes begun by Masaccio in the Carmine Church, Florence; versatile and impressionable, he left many easel pictures of poetic charm. PLATE 13.

LOTTO, Lorenzo (1480–1556), Venetian School; pupil of Giovanni Bellini, friend of Titian, Palma Vecchio, and Aretino; painted religious subjects and portraits. A rich colourist. In 1552 settled at Loreto, dedicating himself and all he possessed to the Santa Casa or Holy House at Loreto, believed to be the house of the Virgin at Nazareth, whence it was transported by the hands of angels in 1294 to the neighbourhood of Recanati. PLATE 31.

MAES, Nicolaes (1632–1693), Dutch School; born at Dordrecht; pupil of Rembrandt; genre painter. PLATE 62.

MANET, Edouard (1832–1883), French School; genre and portrait painter; born in Paris; one of the founders of the Impressionist School. His work aroused bitter hostility on account of its frank directness. Travelled widely, and was strongly influenced by Velazquez. Is now recognized as one of the greatest modern masters. PLATE 95.

MANTEGNA, Andrea (1431–1506), School of Padua; born either at Vicenza or Padua; adopted as a boy by Squarcione, founder of the Paduan School; much influenced by him and Jacopo Bellini; 1454, married Nicolosia, Jacopo's daughter, sister of Giovanni and Gentile Bellini; in 1457 moved to Mantua as court painter to Lodovico Gonzaga; painted religious and historical subjects, austere and sculpturesque in their style. Died at Mantua. PLATE 21.

MARGARITONE d'Arrezo (1216 ?–1293), Tuscan School. Primitive painter, influenced by the Byzantine tradition. The earliest Italian master represented in the National Gallery. PLATE 1.

MEMLING, Hans (1430 ?–1494), Flemish School; lived at Bruges; painted religious subjects with suavity and charm; used the oil methods of the Van Eycks. PLATE 41.

MESSINA, Antonello da (1444–1493), Venetian School; born at Messina, in Sicily, whence his surname; came to Venice, bringing with him a knowledge of the Van Eycks' method of oil painting; painted religious subjects and portraits. Is well represented at the National Gallery. PLATE 24.

METSU, Gabriel (1630–1667), Dutch School; born at Leyden; pupil of Gerard Dou; painter of conversation pieces of outstanding delicacy. PLATE 58.

MICHELANGELO (1475–1564), Florentine School. Sculptor, painter, architect, and poet. One of the world's supreme masters. Surname was Buonarroti. Famous for his frescoes in the Sistine Chapel; built the dome of St. Peter's. Left few easel pictures, two of which are among the treasures of the National Gallery. PLATE 16.

MORETTO (1498 ?–1555 ?), School of Brescia; born at Brescia; real name was Alessandro Bonvicino; known by his nickname " The Blackamoor "; painter of religious subjects and portraits, Titianesque in manner, and distinguished by their silvery colouring. PLATE 30.

MORLAND, George (1763–1804), English School; genre and landscape painter; noted for his animal paintings and scenes of country life. PLATE 75.

ORPEN, Sir William (1878–1931), Irish painter; born in Co. Dublin; portrait and genre painter; selected by the Government to paint pictures of the Great War. Possessed remarkable technical facility. PLATE 92.

PERUGINO (1446–1523), Umbrian School; Pietro Vannucci, born near Perugia, from which he takes the name by which he is generally known, pupil of Fiorenzo di Lorenzo and Verrocchio; religious painter; master of Raphael. PLATE 6.

PINTURICCHIO (1454–1513), Umbrian School; Bernardino di Betto, known by his nickname " The Little Painter "; born at Perugia; painted chiefly in fresco; worked in Rome for Pope Alexander VI. (Borgia); settled in Sienna, where he died by the neglect and starvation, it is said, to which he was abandoned by an infamous wife. PLATE 7.

POLLAIUOLO, Antonio (1432–1498), and Piero (1443–1496), Florentine School; born in Florence; noted for their study of anatomy; had for pupil Verrocchio. Important on technical rather than æsthetic grounds. PLATE 4.

RAEBURN, Sir Henry, R.A. (1756–1823), Scottish portrait painter; born at Edinburgh; travelled in Italy; a sound and honest craftsman. PLATE 74.

RAPHAEL (1483–1520), Umbrian School;

BIOGRAPHICAL INDEX

Raphael Sanzio ; born at Urbino ; apprenticed to Perugino ; 1508, summoned to Rome by Pope Julius II., where he executed frescoes in the Vatican ; his works include oil paintings, frescoes, designs for tapestry, etc.; died at Rome in 1520. PLATES 17, 18.

REMBRANDT (1606–1669), Dutch School ; Rembrandt Van Rijn ; born at Leyden, where his father was a miller ; a highly individualistic painter whose work was informed by an intense humanity, specially noted for his handling of light ; a great etcher ; died at Amsterdam in extreme poverty. PLATES 51, 52, 53.

REYNOLDS, Sir Joshua, P.R.A. (1723–1792), English School ; founder and first president of the Royal Academy ; famous as a portrait painter. PLATES 67, 68, 69.

ROMNEY, George (1734–1802), English School ; born at Beckside, near Dalton-in-Furness ; settled in London, where he became a fashionable portrait painter. PLATES 72, 73.

ROSSETTI, Dante Gabriel (1828–1882), English School ; one of the founders of the pre-Raphaelite Brotherhood ; distinguished as a poet as well as an artist. PLATE 88.

RUBENS, Sir Peter Paul (1577–1640), Flemish School ; studied in Italy, where he entered the service of the Duke of Mantua ; courtier and diplomat ; visited England in 1629, when he was knighted by Charles I. ; superb decorative painter and portraiturist ; master of Van Dyck. PLATES 46, 47, 48.

SEURAT, Georges (1859–1891), French School ; born in Paris ; practised the *pointilliste* method of Impressionism ; painted chiefly in Normandy and on the banks of the Seine ; landscape and genre subjects. PLATE 98.

SICKERT, Richard Walter, R.A. (1860–1942), English School ; much influenced by Impressionism, noted as a colourist. PLATE 94.

STEER, P. Wilson (1860–1942), English School ; equally distinguished as a figure painter and landscapist. PLATE 91.

TERBORCH, Gerard (1617–1681), Dutch School ; born at Zwolle ; travelled widely ; noted for his conversation pieces and portraits. PLATES 54, 55.

TINTORETTO (1518–1594), Venetian School ; Jacopo Robusti ; born in Venice ; the son of a dyer ; known by his nickname "The Little Dyer" ; studied under Titian, and became one of the world's greatest colourists. PLATES 33, 34.

TITIAN (1489 ?–1576), Venetian School ; Tiziano Vecellio ; born at Pieve di Cadore, in mountainous country north of Venice ; studied under Giovanni Bellini ; friend of Giorgione ; one of the greatest painters of all time ; master of El Greco. PLATES 26, 27, 28.

TURNER, Joseph Mallord William (1775–1851), English School ; born in London ; R.A. in 1802 ; travelled in Italy, 1820 ; famous for his water colours, as well as for his oil paintings ; devoted himself to landscape and mythological subjects ; one of the most imaginative of English artists. PLATES 82, 83, 84, 85, 86, 87.

UCCELLO, Paolo (1397–1475), Florentine School ; Paolo di Dono, known by his nickname "Paul of the Birds," because he was extremely fond of them ; famous for his researches into linear perspective. PLATE 2.

VECCHIO, Palma (1480–1528), Venetian School ; Jacopo Palma, known as Palma Vecchio "the Elder" ; born near Bergamo ; pupil of Giovanni Bellini ; painted religious subjects and portraits. PLATE 29.

VELAZQUEZ, Don Diego de Silva y (1599–1660), Spanish School, pupil at Seville of Herrera and Pacheco ; 1623, presented to Philip IV., and later received a court appointment at Madrid ; great as a portrait painter, also painted genre and historical subject-pictures ; his best work is in the Prado at Madrid ; highly sensitive touch ; the greatest Spanish painter. PLATES 64, 65.

VERMEER, Jan (1632–1657), Dutch School ; Jan Vermeer van Delft, famous for his conversation pieces, his studies of Delft ; a subtle colourist who could give a vibrant effect to his handling of light ; his works are scarce and highly prized. PLATE 61.

VERONESE, Paolo (1528–1588), Venetian School ; Paolo Cagliari, born at Verona, hence his name ; came to Venice in 1555, received many commissions from the Doge ; great decorative painter, his large compositions being full of a sumptuous pageantry. PLATE 32.

VINCI, Leonardo da (1452–1519), Florentine School ; illegitimate son of Ser Piero, a notary of Vinci, in the Val d'Arno ; entered the studio of Verrocchio ; 1483, in Milan, where he entered the service of Ludovico Sforza, Duke of Milan ; painter, scientist, engineer, he summed up in himself the culture of his age ; 1498, completed "The Last Supper" in the Dominican Convent of S. Maria delle Grazie in Milan ; 1499, returned to Florence ; commissioned to paint Mona Lisa, wife of Francesco del Giocondo ; spent four years on this work ; 1506, returned to Milan ; invited to France by Francis I., and died near Amboise. One of the greatest minds that have ever lived. PLATE 15.

PLATE I.—MARGARITONE (1216 ?–1293)
TUSCAN SCHOOL

"THE VIRGIN AND CHILD, WITH SCENES FROM THE LIVES OF THE SAINTS"

IN searching for the origins of Italian art, we find that it is derived largely from two sources. One was the Græco-Roman style of the painters of the dying pagan civilization, echoes of which lived on in the primitive frescoes of the Catacombs. The other hailed from Byzantium, where an art, entirely new to the West, had sprung up and set itself to the task of decorating the great basilicas. The medium employed was mosaic. It possessed the great merit of permanency, and offered a magnificence in colouring unsurpassed by any other. It had, however, certain limitations. The Byzantine artist was restricted to very bold and massive contours. All minute and detailed treatment of facial expression, for example, or of anatomical realism was precluded. It remained, as it had begun, a hieratic art, ceremonial and remote, but none the less one of the most impressive man has ever achieved.

This altar frontal, the earliest Italian work in the gallery, shows very distinctly the Byzantine influence. It is formal in its design. There is the background of gold. The Madonna sits rigidly, enclosed in a mandorla or almond-shaped glory. The Child is a diminutive man rather than an infant, His hand raised in the conventional attitude of benediction.

But one can trace other influences. There is a quaint vividness in the treatment of the Lives of the Saints suggestive of the old Græco-Roman tempera-painters. Even the Madonna's face is faintly reminiscent of classical portraiture. She might be an august Roman matron. But for the rest Byzantinism reigns complete.

An immense gulf separates this early work from our next illustration. Duccio and Giotto were to come. Duccio, in whom the Byzantine tradition reached its final and crowning achievement in paint ; and Giotto, whose genius was too great and too humanistic to be confined in the older forms. He, more than any other, laid down the lines along which subsequent Italian painting was to develop.

PLATE 1.—THE VIRGIN AND CHILD, WITH SCENES FROM THE LIVES OF
THE SAINTS : Margaritone.

PLATE 2.—PAOLO UCCELLO (1397-1475)
FLORENTINE SCHOOL

"THE ROUT OF SAN ROMANO"

IN the history of art, Florence of the fifteenth century is like a sun, radiating out an intense energy. It was not only that she was the prolific mother of great men. There was something unique in the spirit which animated their minds. A philosophic bent, a love of knowledge for its own sake, an eager curiosity, and the desire to experiment which is at the root of all science.

Following on Giotto, Masaccio had solved the problem of representing objects in the round, of conveying a sense of their mass and volume. He had already apprehended the possibilities of perspective in so far as they concerned his own rather simple and statuesque compositions, and his successors were to extend his discoveries in other directions.

With Uccello indeed the study of linear perspective became almost an obsession. In this painting we can see him exploiting it with all the eagerness of a child playing with a new toy. Look at what one is almost tempted to call the " floor " of the picture, and the broken lances, the recumbent figures lying end-on, their bodies foreshortened, show how he was preoccupied with the new device.

His love of geometry can be seen in the deliberately formal treatment of the hillside. He has simplified its structure into a series of inclined planes. Like the later day " cubists " he was obviously working on a preconceived mathematical idea.

It is impossible, however, to dismiss this picture as a mere technical exercise. It is brimful of pictorial interest. The vigour of the charge has been realized with astounding spirit. And how beautiful is the pattern woven by the whirling standards and the serrated lances. Velasquez must have had it in mind when he painted " The Surrender of Breda."

All sorts of odd experiments in pigment are essayed. Earlier painters were familiar with the use of gold as a ground for transparent colour. Uccello summons silver to his aid. Sir Charles Holmes has an interesting note on this. " Silver foil glazed with black gives a most lively rendering of plate armour and chain mail ; glazed with other colours it endows them with properties which they never possessed before." He draws attention to Uccello's " sense of the value of interchanged tinctures," and " his daring oppositions of quaint shapes and colours and metals." Such in themselves would make this picture remarkable. It is the way these subtleties are all subordinated to the æsthetic sense which gives it its perennial charm.

PLATE 2.—THE ROUT OF SAN ROMANO: Uccello.

PLATE 3.—PIERO DELLA FRANCESCA (1415 ?–1492)
FLORENTINE SCHOOL

" THE NATIVITY "

YOUNGER than Uccello, of whom he was the contemporary, Piero della Francesca carried on that eager spirit of investigation which is such a mark of the Florentine School. His absorbing aim was that of giving his figures solidity, of investing them with the monumental grandeur to which Masaccio had pointed the way.

This preference for sculptural form is inherent in the work of nearly all the great Italian masters. It assisted them in solving the problem which confronts every artist; that is, how to translate the multitudinous forms presented by Nature into the clear statements of such which are demanded by Art. The practice of sculpture leads directly to one of the most satisfactory solutions, for the sculptor is compelled to work in large and clearly defined masses, rejecting the unessentials, and concentrating upon those formal absolutes which give a coherent clarity to his work. To achieve this in painting was the constant preoccupation of Piero.

And so these figures in " The Nativity " have a statuesque definition. They are palpably solid, and the sculptural illusion is heightened by the pale and ashen colours he employs. Even the flesh tints have a marmoreal quality.

One result of this method we may as well notice from the outset. This formal discipline has an important effect. It detaches, as it were, the subject of the picture from its background, just as it emancipates the work itself from the confusing actualities which assail the painter when he looks at life. It is a result of Choice. In all the earlier Italian masters the background of their pictures really *is* a background, remote from the plane of action, with which it is related only by æsthetic considerations. From this comes a restfulness and feeling of quiet concentration. It is in this picture.

Piero here is in one of his gentle moods. His design flows in subtle curving sweeps. Notice the rhythm of the carpet of herbage in the foreground, and how it is taken up in that of the Virgin's robe. His treatment of the subject is very typical. He always evokes a feeling of suspended action, a pause in the drama, infinitely solemn, in which the participants become, as it were, mysterious spectators of the scene they are enacting. A similar note is in his magnificent " Baptism " which hangs on the same wall.

Together they constitute two of the most precious pictures we possess.

PLATE 3.—THE NATIVITY: Piero della Francesca.

PLATE 4.—ANTONIO POLLAIUOLO (1432–1498) AND PIERO POLLAIUOLO (1443–1496)
FLORENTINE SCHOOL

"THE MARTYRDOM OF ST. SEBASTIAN"

UCCELLO and Piero della Francesca were both accomplished mathematicians. Now we come to two other Florentine scientists, Antonio Pollaiuolo and his brother Piero. Their particular bent was anatomy. They set themselves to arrive at an understanding of the movements of the human body by a study of the bones and tendons and muscles. Vasari says that Antonio was the first to make use of the dissection of dead bodies to further his knowledge. Later on, Leonardo was to be absorbed in the same pursuit, carrying his researches into the complex motions that give rise to the play of facial expression. As pioneers the Pollaiuoli did not push their investigation to such an extreme of subtlety. They were concerned with the articulation of joints and tendons as revealed in ordinary physical action.

A glance at "The Martyrdom of St. Sebastian" is sufficient to show their intense interest in this subject. The group of six crossbow-men exhibits the human body in an amazing variety of action. No gesture seems to be too violent, no contortion too involved, to escape recording. Notice with what firmness the four figures in the foreground are depicted. One can feel them bracing themselves, their feet securely planted, their limbs strung to a tautness like a bow itself.

(By way of contrast, it is interesting to look at Pinturicchio's young herald in "The Return of Ulysses" [Plate 7]. His body is so devoid of any articulation that it is inconceivable he could even stand up.)

The Pollaiuoli, by their application of anatomy to painting, left a legacy of knowledge at the disposal of all subsequent artists. But when this is said, one is forced to admit that in their own work their discoveries were often pushed to an excess. The faces, for example, in this picture, writhe and grimace in a kind of barbaric frenzy. The design, too, lacks felicity. The intended circular grouping of the archers round the central figure is broken by conflicting attitudes which interrupt its rhythm. The landscape, despite its elaboration, remains a dull and uninspiring statement.

It is interesting to note that this picture has been painted in oils. Antonio was one of the earliest to use this medium in place of tempera, where the colour was mixed with the yolk of egg and water. Lack of experience in the new process accounts for the darkening of the pigment with age, and robs this picture of any distinctive chromatic appeal. Its importance, however, in the field of anatomical research cannot be over-estimated.

4

PLATE 4.—THE MARTYRDOM OF ST. SEBASTIAN: Pollaiuolo.

PLATE 5.—FRA FILIPPO LIPPI (1406 ?–1469)
FLORENTINE SCHOOL

"ST. JOHN THE BAPTIST WITH SIX OTHER SAINTS"

FRA FILIPPO LIPPI cannot be accused of being a scientist. The story of his abduction of the nun Lucrezia Buti, and of his subsequent marriage to her, is too well known to need recapitulation. It is of double interest because of their union was born the painter Filippino Lippi, and because it throws a light upon his character, revealing him as a man to whom real men and women were of more account than any abstract theory. As we might expect, he did not contribute any startling innovation to Florentine painting. He was content to accept the current traditions as he found them, yet his personality was so marked that it is stamped indelibly on his work, the sign-manual of which is an intimate humanity.

Look at this lunette (*i.e.* moon-shaped) picture and you can see at once that his saints are no mere hierarchical personages. They are creatures of flesh and blood, very definitely "characters," and their conversation would not appear to consist of the traditional "yea or nay," but rather partakes of the nature of (shall we say, celestial ?) gossip. They are happily ensconced in a pleasant garden seat, and if one or two bear evidences of rather harrowing ordeals (*e.g.* St. Lawrence, second from the left with his gridiron) they are not unduly discomfited, nor do they disturb us.

Fra Lippo Lippi's real contribution to painting consists in his use of colour. His agreeably sensuous nature inclined him to this. His predecessors had confined their palette to rather simple and unmixed tones. They used them with a breadth of direct luminosity that satisfied their needs. Fra Lippo Lippi begins a process of delicate nuance. His spectrum dissolves. His reds are no longer absolute reds, they take on all sorts of intermediate hues. The same subtle transitions are apparent in all the other shades.

The effect is one of warmth, of pleasing gradations of tone, surprisingly sophisticated when contrasted with the direct precision of his contemporaries. One critic goes so far as to say that we have to wait for Watteau before colour refinements of the same kind occur again.

PLATE 5.—ST. JOHN THE BAPTIST WITH SIX OTHER SAINTS :
Fra Filippo Lippi.

PLATE 6.—PIETRO PERUGINO (1446-1523)

UMBRIAN SCHOOL

"THE VIRGIN ADORING THE INFANT CHRIST"

WE shall return to Florence to greet the mature personality of Botticelli, but for the moment we might well cast an eye over the work that is being done outside her walls. Perugia is one of the towns we must visit, and in Perugino we come face to face with its master painter. He takes his name from the little city in the Umbrian hills. After Florence and Sienna it was one of the most important centres of art. Its picturesque situation in an upland country, where the eye was accustomed to wide and aerial vistas, had much to do in moulding the art of Perugino, who is particularly noted for his pure and tranquil colouring (especially his blues) and for his treatment of space. These qualities are revealed very clearly in this picture.

The Madonna is seen adoring her sacred Child, who is presented to her in the arms of an attendant angel. The rich blue of their draperies, contrasted with the warm flesh tints and deep rose in the Virgin's attire, makes a most harmonious passage of colour. Not less lovely is the serene and restful landscape which extends beyond.

Perugino had this gift of leading the eye to an almost infinite recession of distance. His landscapes become his figures with a felicity that has seldom been equalled. The tall, feathery trees add to this suggestion of space, and the horizon, when it is reached, sleeps, like a sea almost, against the purity of the sky.

How consummate is his rendering of this wide expanse can be seen at once when we look at the figures of the three angels. They are conventional enough in their gestures, but they actually *are* floating in space. In fact, they seem to soar. Only a great master could have achieved this miracle.

After such praise it is perhaps unkind to detect certain mannerisms, a possibly affected pietism, inclined to rapt attitudes bordering on the theatrical. They were fresh when they first came from his hand, but Perugino was rather prone to their repetition, and they have been used so often since that they end by becoming insipid.

Perugino had for pupil the youthful Raphael, upon whom he exercised a very definite influence. That alone would make him memorable, but the works of his mature period are a sufficient monument in themselves.

PLATE 6.—THE VIRGIN ADORING THE INFANT CHRIST: Perugino.

PLATE 7.—PINTURICCHIO (1454–1513)
UMBRIAN SCHOOL

"THE RETURN OF ULYSSES"

PINTURICCHIO, "the little painter," was, like Perugino, one of those masters who have shed lustre upon the Umbrian hill-town of his birth. He was born at Perugia in 1454. This interesting fresco, "The Return of Ulysses," reveals both his charm and his limitations. It is full of a bustling animation, the action being depicted with touches of vivid realism.

Penelope is seated on the left, the bow and quiver of her long-absent lord hanging above her head. She is at work on the tapestry with which she occupied herself and delayed the advances of her suitors. On the floor at her side a girl is winding thread on to shuttles from a ball of yarn with which a cat is playing. The upright frame of the loom very cleverly divides the picture into two sections. Advancing towards the centre, a young herald announces the return of the hero. Two of the suitors on the right do not seem to receive the news with any great pleasure. One of them, a dandified young man, carrying a hawk on his wrist, is the personification of the listless philanderer. The other, wearing a turban, accepts the inevitable with a rather morose expression. Ulysses himself is seen entering by the door on the right. The pattern on the floor and the lines of the loom very skilfully lead one's gaze to the harbour scene beyond, where the flamboyant ship is dropping anchor, and a boat is coming to shore under a castellated cliff.

Nothing has been omitted, and the picture abounds with a hundred and one minutely observed details. This indeed gives it considerable charm, but one cannot help feeling that it is over-crowded. There is an uneasy sense of confusion in the design, and when we come to study the fresco more closely, we see that the figures lack substance. They are decorative, not real. The young herald in the foreground might almost have been cut out of cardboard. He has no bones or sinews or semblance of any solidity whatsoever.

Pinturicchio never visited Florence. Possibly that may account for this deficiency. And yet he must have seen the work of Piero della Francesca. However that may be, he chose to busy himself by exploiting his decorative facility, and so remains, as he was born, a provincial, just a little bit outside of the vital currents of art.

PLATE 7.—THE RETURN OF ULYSSES: Pinturicchio.

PLATE 8.—FRANCESCO FRANCIA (1450-1517)
SCHOOL OF BOLOGNA

"PIETÀ"

FRANCESCO FRANCIA, greatest of the Bolognese painters, received his training from a goldsmith and was famous throughout Italy as a designer of coins and medals. One of the qualities he thus acquired was that of adapting his subjects to fit into the shapes, especially the circular ones, demanded by that craft.

Bologna, lying between the Tuscan and Venetian territories, was subject to influences from North and South alike, a fact which contributed to the eclectic nature of Francia's art. He had much in common with the Umbrians, especially Perugino.

This lunette forms the upper portion of an altar-piece, the lower panel of which represents the Madonna with St. Anne, surrounded by saints. It is the most beautiful section of the work and has received the admiration of successive generations. The dead body of Christ lies across the knees of His mother, His head supported gently by the angel on the left, while another with clasped hands is gazing on His wounded feet.

The design is singularly fluent and attractive. It is adapted most skilfully to the exigencies required by the space. Notice how the curving, crescent wings of the angels, and the soft, grey halo of the Virgin placed at the apex of the arc, contribute to this harmony. The long diagonal line of the body of Christ introduces a counter-rhythm, delicate, gentle, undulating, and its note of tenderness is echoed in the forms of the angels and the mourning Madonna.

The colouring is pleasing and effective, its reds and greens, its ivories and sombre blues, even its dusky greys, all seen most clearly against the darkness of their ground.

Yet, when this is said, one feels that there is something lacking. It is too studied, too deliberately conscious in its art. (This is a fault liable to beset all eclecticism.) Perugino's slight theatricality is here carried a stage further on its decline from convincing power. Set this beside one of the primitive Pietàs and its lack of profound passion is at once apparent. To a certain type of mind, however, what is in reality a defect not infrequently passes as a virtue.

PLATE 8.—PIETÀ : Francia.

PLATE 9.—SANDRO BOTTICELLI (1444–1510)
FLORENTINE SCHOOL

" PORTRAIT OF A YOUNG MAN "

BOTTICELLI is now recognized as one of the most individual and engaging personalities in the history of art. Yet before Ruskin began to draw attention to his quality, in England, at any rate, he had been all but forgotten. The enthusiasm which marked the rediscovery of his genius was inclined to dwell upon the more obvious and " poetic " aspects of his painting, and his name became associated with an often over-effusive sentimentality.

For that reason we cannot do better than begin with this extremely simple and direct portrait. It is the earliest work of his we happen to possess, and it shows quite unmistakably his passionate sincerity and purity of line. Reveals, too, a certain grave strength and quality of repose, apt to be overlooked in his more elaborate compositions.

Why is this picture so hauntingly vivid ? It is painted in very quiet and sombre tones, the only high spots of colour being the red of the cap and the white braid on the coat. There is no attempt at any dramatic expression. The secret of this portrait lies in the clear and purposeful manner in which Botticelli has seen his subject, and in the incisive mastery of line with which he has set his vision down.

He had learned much of anatomy from the study of Pollaiuolo, by whom he was considerably influenced, and he has here put his knowledge to use in the exquisite modelling of the face.

Begin with the eyes and the delicately painted eyebrows, and pass on to the sensitive nostrils and the firm crescent of the lips. Then notice the wide contour of the head as a whole, framed in its flowing arabesque of locks. It is replete with a demure yet fully realized vitality.

People of that age (the early Renaissance) seem to have possessed a certain quality in which the soul or the mind (call it what you will) was inextricably bound up with the flesh. Their lineaments appear to us much more expressive of the real personality than do those of succeeding generations.

It may be mere fantasy to think so, but if it is, it is one that has been created by works of art such as this portrait we have been looking upon.

9

PLATE 9.—PORTRAIT OF A YOUNG MAN: Botticelli.

PLATE 10.—SANDRO BOTTICELLI (1444–1510)
FLORENTINE SCHOOL

"THE VIRGIN AND CHILD"

THIS work reveals another aspect of Botticelli's many-sided genius. He was a complex personality. The ferment of the Renaissance was working in his veins, its re-discovered paganism striving with the Catholic tradition. Often they were very curiously blent and intermixed in his work. It is hard to say which was nearest to his heart ; whether he loved most his Venus rising from the sea, or the wistful Madonna faces he painted so often. Probably it is truest to say that after his own fashion he was faithful to them both ; for his Venus in that radiant moment of her apparition wears a gentle sadness, her flesh already troubled with a soul, and his Madonnas are a type of their own, sensitive, delicate, rather listless, burdened by a mystery they do not comprehend, and from which they are not a little detached.

The Madonna in this tondo (*i.e.* circular) picture is an example of the type he loved to portray. Pale, fair, elaborately attired, nursing her Divine Infant, yet at the same time looking as though her thoughts were very far away. She is not human, neither is she transfigured by any profoundly religious fire. The two attendant figures incline towards her in a remote and silent tenderness. Especially beautiful is the head of St. John the Baptist on the left. With a complete disregard for realism he is depicted as much older than the Saviour, and has the delicate and almost girlish features of a Florentine page-boy of the time.

The least satisfactory figure is the Child. He is clumsily drawn, and there are defects, too, in the anatomy of the other bodies, which suggest that this work was probably executed in part by pupils.

But the depth of feeling, the types portrayed, and the features of the design are so essentially the products of Botticelli's genius, that it must have been painted under his direct supervision. Not otherwise could it convey so much of his poetry and intimate personal charm.

PLATE 10.—THE VIRGIN AND CHILD: Botticelli.

PLATE 11.—SANDRO BOTTICELLI (1444–1510)
FLORENTINE SCHOOL

"THE NATIVITY"

IN his later years Botticelli came under the influence of Savonarola, who had raised the standard of a fiery puritanism against the pagan luxury and corruption of his age. Moved by the preaching of the great Friar, he renounced the world, and, if we are to believe Vasari, fell into a religious melancholy which lasted until his death in 1510.

This rapturous "Nativity," painted not long after Savonarola's martyrdom, shows, however, that the fervour of faith could move him to heights he has seldom excelled.

One is aware of an overwhelming excitement in this work, which expresses itself in an infinite variety of movement. The Angelic Choir against their vivid sky of gold and palest azure carry this passionate rhythm to an extreme. Not even the dancers in his " Primavera " evoke such ethereal lightness. It is unique in the annals of art.

But this movement is everywhere : in the figures of angels and men who embrace in the foreground. They seem to fly into each other's arms. (The three humans are supposed to represent Savonarola and the two fellow-monks, Fra Silvestro and Fra Domenico, who shared his martyrdom.)

The rocky crevices with their zigzag pattern like streaks of lightning, the rush of grey volcanic stone forming the ramparts of the cave, translate this amazing vigour into the forms of earth itself. The shepherds and the Magi hasten with their escort of angels to lay their adoration at the inner shrine of the picture, where alone there is repose. (Yet even the draperies of the sleeping St. Joseph are contorted with the same frenzy.)

The handling of this passionate *allégresse* affects one like a complicated piece of music. Its subtleties are innumerable, and the eye can return again and again without exhausting its content.

In this quality Botticelli was unique. If, as we have reason to believe, this was the last picture he painted, his art ended on the note it most triumphantly proclaims.

PLATE 11.—THE NATIVITY: Botticelli.

PLATE 12.—DOMENICO GHIRLANDAIO (1449-1494)
FLORENTINE SCHOOL

"PORTRAIT OF A GIRL"

GHIRLANDAIO, the contemporary of Botticelli, derives his name from the fact that he was apprenticed to a goldsmith whose speciality was the making of jewelled coronals (*ghirlande*), much in favour with Florentine ladies of the period. He was unquestionably an artist of great talent, and his frescoes, particularly those depicting scenes from the lives of St. John the Baptist and the Virgin, which are among the chief treasures of the church of Santa Maria Novella in Florence, show that he possessed a power of design and execution notable even in that city of notabilities.

The Louvre possesses two of his most outstanding easel pictures, " The Visitation " and " The Bottle-nosed Man and a Child." The former has a gracious poetic charm, while the latter reveals him as a realist who could paint a wrinkled and, at first sight, rather repulsive subject, and yet endow it with a tenderness that fills the whole work with humanity.

We are not so fortunate as the Louvre, but this " Portrait of a Girl " is strikingly fresh and attractive, and would not pass unnoticed in any gallery.

She is seen in three-quarter face, her fair wavy hair rippling down to her shoulders. There is no attempt at high relief, and the flesh tints have been subdued to a delicate ivory, whose purity is emphasized by the crimson necklace she is wearing, and by the fainter rose-pink of her lips. The whole figure is sharply silhouetted against a dark background. He has very skilfully utilized the lock of hair curling down over her left cheek to soften the contrast between light and dark, which otherwise might have been too abrupt. Her dress is treated simply, the scarlet bodice with its white fillet of beads and full greenish sleeves fitting admirably into the picture.

One thinks of Horace's maiden " *simplex munditiis*," " plain in thy neatness " as Milton has rendered it. But if she is neat in person and attire, she has her full share of the beauty of youth, and it is this naïve and vividly realized charm that gives this portrait its undeniable appeal.

12

PLATE 12.—PORTRAIT OF A GIRL: Ghirlandaio.

PLATE 13.—FILIPPINO LIPPI (1457-1504), FLORENTINE SCHOOL

"THE VIRGIN AND CHILD WITH ST. JEROME AND ST. DOMINIC"

FILIPPINO LIPPI, the son of the painter Fra Filippo Lippi, was one of the most brilliant pupils of Botticelli. As was only natural, his work was considerably influenced by that master. He was, indeed, impressionable rather than original, and his tastes inclined him to a somewhat emasculate loveliness. It is apparent in his delight in elaborate and flower-like drapery, and in his preference for a certain type of physical delicacy in the figures he painted. This over-refinement, however, is not without its compensating charm. It was a tendency of the time, and even the greatest masters did not wish to avoid it. One thinks of the passionate tenderness with which Leonardo painted the angel in his "Virgin of the Rocks," and of the entwining hands of Michelangelo's two exquisite youths in the "Madonna and St. John."

In an artist of lesser genius such a predilection was not without its dangers, and it is not difficult to trace various influences, echoes of style from other painters, in this work. The face of the Madonna and her exquisitely painted veil might be by Botticelli. Sir Charles Holmes suggests Leonardo as the source of the rugged battlement of rocks to the left of the picture, and detects his influence in the rather surprising anatomical vigour of the St. Jerome. But however this may be, all critics are agreed that Filippino has succeeded in fusing these possibly derivative passages into a singularly effective whole.

The beauty and individuality of the colouring alone would suffice to give this picture its distinction. Notice how he has employed deep masses of black, contrasted with the palest of ivory, and how the browns are relieved with touches of pure gold which shine like a faint autumnal sun in the halo of the Virgin.

Filippino's delicacy of feeling is apparent everywhere, in the foliage of the tree whose leaves are outlined against the sky, in the lily of St. Dominic, blossoming like the flower of the Annunciation, and shedding its sweetness upon his pale ascetic head, and most of all in the almost disembodied radiance of the Madonna.

She is drawn with a purity of line and disregard for high modelling or relief that convey impressions evoked by Oriental art, and show a curious and quite inadvertent similarity in style to that of Chinese painting.

One is aware of a profound and haunting emotion that has here taken complete possession of all Filippino's preciousness, and given to his sensitivity a reward that is all the more surprising because one might have expected less.

13

PLATE 13.—THE VIRGIN AND CHILD, WITH ST. JEROME AND ST. DOMINIC:
Filippino Lippi.

PLATE 14.—PIERO DI COSIMO (1462-1521)

FLORENTINE SCHOOL

"THE DEATH OF PROCRIS"

AFTER the saints, the satyrs; after the martyrdoms, the piteous tragedies of human passion—no less human because cloaked in a mythological disguise. Cephalus, the goat-footed, has slain by mischance Procris whom he loved, and is bent in sorrow over her head, while his dog looks on with a sympathy equally intense.

The Renaissance with its re-discovery of pagan myth accounts for this—accounts for it, at least, as a subject—but does not wholly account for the intimate way in which Piero di Cosimo has depicted the scene.

He was somewhat of a recluse, a shy and individualistic painter, living apart, his mind peopled with the phantasms and monsters that stirred the imagination of the classical age. It is beside the point to mention that he was a contemporary of the greatest Florentines. He owed little to them. In technical achievement he was probably their inferior, but he had his own outlook on the world, and it is in this picture. It is one of the most lovely we possess.

In shape it is remarkable: a long narrow panel with the recumbent Procris occupying the foreground, and the two sombre forms of satyr and of dog bent over her corpse. Cephalus was a hunter and went out daily to the woods. Procris fondly imagined that he was unfaithful to her, and inflamed with jealousy, hid herself in a thicket. Seeing the leaves stirring he surmised the presence of a quarry and let his arrow fly. That is the story. It is sad enough.

If this picture does not reveal it all, it is not for lack of Cosimo's penetration. Nor, like the classics, would he end on a note of grief. He carries the eye beyond to an exquisite landscape: the shore quick with animal life, the estuary with its birds on wing, and its pale blue receding forelands.

D. H. Lawrence must have liked this picture. It is full of the vivid animalistic feeling that he loved. The brown earthy tones of the satyr, stooping in ineffectual (and for that reason, all the more poignant) sorrow, would have gone to his heart. So would the dog.

"We may value," says Sir Charles Holmes, "Piero's fantasy all the more, because this is the last glimpse we get of such a thing in Florence."

After him were to come the giants.

PLATE 14.—THE DEATH OF PROCRIS : Cosimo.

PLATE 15.—LEONARDO DA VINCI (1452–1519)
FLORENTINE SCHOOL

"THE VIRGIN OF THE ROCKS"

THIS strange and solemn picture cannot be adequately dealt with in a few words. Leonardo's genius is so complex, so indisputably great, that any work of his has a profundity not to be extracted in a passing glance. In his person were summed up all the science and learning of his age, and added to this was a power of creating beauty that has never been equalled. When he has drawn a line we feel as if a mysterious virtue had passed into it from himself. Every brush-stroke has a similar miraculous quality.

This sensitivity was not attained without an immense amount of work. He had observed and studied all the subtle movements in the play of facial expression, every refinement of the flesh that gives one a delineation of the soul.

The result is the delicacy we can see in his portrayal of the Madonna, and of the angel by her side. How beautiful is the outstretched hand, the rhythm that caresses face and hair and neck, and sweeps in a gentle curve down to the infant Christ. Here this indwelling intensity is carried almost too far. It is unbelievable that any child could convey the depth of feeling expressed in His grave prophetic benediction. Such a tenderness trembles on the verge where reality passes beyond the limits of the seen.

His method of painting had its attendant dangers. In his desire to give his figures a relief no less real than that of nature itself, he had recourse to the use of dark shadows. The technique of oil painting was not at this time fully understood, and as a result his pigments have darkened, obliterating in an increasing gloom much delicate detail. That in part explains the opaque impenetrability of much of this picture.

One word has to be said of the mysterious background. Leonardo had an intense interest in geology. He studied the formations of rock, and had arrived at an understanding of the immense vistas of geological time. This landscape is that of a primæval age, when the seas washed the bases of the mountains, and the basaltic tumult had not yet abated. Did he desire to remind us that the Child in this picture was He of whom it was said that He was " begotten of His Father before all worlds "? If he wished to, he could not have done it more marvellously.

PLATE 15.—THE VIRGIN OF THE ROCKS: Leonardo da Vinci.

PLATE 16.—MICHELANGELO (1475-1564)

FLORENTINE SCHOOL

"THE ENTOMBMENT"

ONE quality Michelangelo and Leonardo possessed in common. It is simple to call it genius, but that word has been so much degraded by indiscriminate use that it does little to convey the sense of glory it should possess when applied to these two masters. All that Florence at the height of her greatness could give them they had. By one of those rare and fortunate chances of fate, their very names both by sound and derivation seem designed for fame.

Of the two, Michelangelo was made of sterner stuff. He was a sculptor born and bred, and the discipline of the rock never left him. As a painter his power can only be realized by those who have visited the Sistine Chapel. As an architect, he has left the dome of St. Peter's an eternal witness of his strength.

Only three easel pictures are ascribed to him, and of these our National Gallery possesses two. It is a unique distinction.

"The Entombment," despite its unfinished condition, gives us an insight into the mastery at his command. The formal composition of this picture is so important that it must be dealt with. The body of Christ, placed in a central position, fixes the attention by its dead staggering weight. Such a rhythm could not live unsupported. It is balanced on the left by the massive diagonal of St. John, and on the right by the bow-like figure of St. Mary Magdalene, who, like counter-subjects in music, answer and support the original theme. But such a vertical composition of crescent-shaped inclining forms might not be able to stand by itself. And so Michelangelo has introduced an unsuspected counter-rhythm. It begins with the head of Salome sitting on the left, is continued by the girdle across the thighs of St. John, and the line of hands (all on one level) leading to the unfinished blank which, filled in, would have been a representation of the Virgin.

Instead of the perilous chiaroscuro of Leonardo, with its obliterating shadows, the illusion of relief is given by an almost miraculous modelling, carried out with an amazing economy of tone, especially in the flesh tints. These forms possess a marmoreal definition, and to this is added a bold and spacious use of colour which, in itself, would make Michelangelo a master in this field.

It is an early work, but already in the massive figure of St. John we can see the mind which created the demi-gods of the Sistine ceiling.

PLATE 16.—THE ENTOMBMENT: Michelangelo.

PLATE 17.—RAPHAEL (1483–1520)
UMBRIAN SCHOOL

"THE VIRGIN AND CHILD, WITH ST. JOHN THE BAPTIST AND ST. NICHOLAS"

OF Raphael it had at once be better said that his best work can only be seen in Rome. He enjoys, or rather endures, an invidious position in art. His name is so often upon the lips of those who have only seen him at second-best, that when we try to estimate his greatness we are beset with the difficulty that the works which have most commonly been cited as his title to celebrity are precisely those in which his full genius has failed to find its expression.

In Rome, and in contact with the Sistine greatness of Michelangelo, his consummate powers of pictorial logic reached a plenitude that ranks him among the masters of all time. Such are his frescoes in the Vatican, "The School of Athens" for example, or "The Mass of Bolsena." In London the cartoon of "The Miraculous Draught of Fishes" at South Kensington exhibits his maturity to a greater degree than any easel picture at Trafalgar Square.

With this in mind we can proceed to a consideration of the works illustrated in the two succeeding plates.

The picture of "The Virgin and Child, attended by St. John the Baptist and St. Nicholas of Bari" (commonly known as the "Ansidei Madonna"), was painted for Perugia, and in it Raphael is much influenced by Perugino, under whom he studied. Perugino had painted a "Holy Family with St. Anne," which Raphael must have had in his mind's eye when he began this work. He improved upon it, however. The sky beyond the archway has an ethereal lightness that is his own, and the very formal throne upon which the Virgin is seated is less heavy than Perugino's. Such inventions as the pendent chains of coral beads which break the sharpness of its outline are refinements of Raphael's own sensitivity. The figure of St. Nicholas with his book and crozier has a solidity and definition which is Florentine in its manner. Less happy is the somewhat theatrical attitude of St. John. There, one is aware of a rather conscious dramatic exaggeration. The Madonna and Child are decidedly conventional, and the whole picture has a stiffness and symmetrical rectitude which give little scope for any surprising originality.

For his more magical effects we must turn to our next illustration.

PLATE 17.—THE VIRGIN AND CHILD, WITH ST. JOHN THE BAPTIST AND
ST. NICHOLAS: Raphael.

PLATE 18.—RAPHAEL (1483–1520)
UMBRIAN SCHOOL

"THE MADONNA OF THE TOWER"

SO different is this picture from our last that one would be pardoned for attributing it to another master. It is the most beautiful Raphael we possess. Since painting the " Ansidei Madonna " he had been to Rome, and his work there, as we have remarked, took on a plenitude, a width of conception, which is his enduring title to fame. The freedom that came to him then, the formal yet very human passion, are here expressed with an exquisite intimacy. At first sight neither the Madonna nor her substantial Child are distinctly celestial. But such tenderness of feeling, such maternal solicitude, such implicit childish affection grow by a subtle interplay of emotion into a relationship which is as divine as it is human.

The grouping of the figures builds up an impressive pyramidal form. Even the gentle descent of the veil, despite its over-painting, contributes to this effect. As a counter-rhythm the embracing hands and arms knit together the composition, binding the Child and mother in the most spontaneous of gestures.

Equally happy is the colouring; the glowing flesh tints, the diffused golden lights in the hair, the Virgin's attire, silvery-grey of the mantle, (in the original it is tinged with lilac), the crimson of her sleeve, and the profound nocturnal blue beneath, all contribute to a luminous harmony which was new then and still preserves its magic.

The sombre and sympathetic landscape deserves, as it invites, an attention which cannot be dismissed with a cursory notice.

Perugino, for all his wizardry of ethereal extension, never set such figures against such a romantic expanse. The forms of earth are here subdued to a gracious harmony, remote, yet allied to the beings that dominate their distances. No detail distracts. The eye is free to rove from the wide plain to the heaven suffused with snowy clouds. Set beside the violence of Mantegna's backgrounds, or the naïve definition of the primitives, the sense of liberation is complete and entrancing. To it this picture owes not a little of its power to enthral.

PLATE 18.—THE MADONNA OF THE TOWER: Raphael.

PLATE 19.—CORREGGIO (1494–1534)
SCHOOL OF PARMA

"MERCURY INSTRUCTING CUPID IN THE PRESENCE OF VENUS"

WITH Leonardo and Michelangelo the greatness of Florence reached its zenith. After that it began to wane. Political unrest had much to do with this. Leonardo spent a great part of his time in Milan, Michelangelo in Rome. Raphael was an Umbrian. We are approaching the age when Venice was to gather to itself the last rich flowering of the classical Italian Schools, but before we reach that island city we have pauses to make on our way. Our journey, however, takes us north; our faces are set in the direction of that goal.

Correggio, the greatest painter of the Parmese School, was but ten years the junior of Raphael. We do not know much about his early training. He was a painter who achieved fame more by his own native gifts and genius than by conscious study of his predecessors. Unlike the great Florentines, he had no ambition to probe to the innermost core of things. He painted many religious subjects, but they affect us by their pleasant humanity rather than by any spiritual depth.

This picture reveals very clearly his proclivities. He was happiest in his works that were inspired by the re-discovered paganism. In his great decorations for the dome of St. Giovanni at Parma, the apostles are painted in the nude. They recline in attitudes portrayed with an amazing command of foreshortening, like Olympian Titans rather than Christian saints.

His easel pictures incline to a softer and more voluptuous manner. He was quick to seize upon the possibilities of the new medium of oil-paint. He discovered that it could be used with a greater fluency and in far more body than had hitherto been attempted, and thereby laid the foundations of modern practice. With it came an increasing use of chiaroscuro to give his figures relief. In this picture the background is so dark that they seem almost to have been conceived in the round. The old bright precision of tempera-painting is lost, and instead we have the sensuality of shade as a foil to his glowing treatment of the flesh.

Much attention has been paid to the silvery whiteness and delicacy in the painting of Cupid's wing and Mercury's headpiece. The whole picture is strikingly modern in the effect. It might have been painted in the eighteenth century, and it comes almost like a shock when we remember that in reality it is over four hundred years old.

PLATE 19.—MERCURY INSTRUCTING CUPID: Correggio.

PLATE 20.—GIOVANNI BOLTRAFFIO (1467-1516)
SCHOOL OF MILAN

"PORTRAIT OF A MAN"

BOLTRAFFIO was one of a group of artists, mostly Milanese in origin, whose style was largely formed by the example of Leonardo da Vinci. Leonardo went to Milan in 1482, where he entered the service of Ludovico Sforza, remaining in that city until 1499, when he returned to Florence. It was only natural that round him should gather a school of painters inspired by his greatness, but the truth is that when we come to examine their contribution to the history of art we meet with a disappointment. Leonardo was so great that he was a dangerous master to take for model. Their admiration for him led them into attempted imitation, and it is impossible to imitate Leonardo. Achievement such as his could only be attained by an immense amount of original research and patient hard labour, never to speak of the possession of outstanding genius. He offered no short-cut to success, and the so-called " School of Leonardo " is a warning that imitators cannot expect to produce master-pieces of the first order.

This is not to say that their works are negligible. The instance of Il Sodoma, perhaps the most talented of Leonardo's followers, should prevent us from any too sweeping generalizations, and Boltraffio, as we can see from this striking picture, was among other things a portrait-painter of no mean ability.

Its prevailing note is one of gravity. The incisive profile, severe in its drawing, the studied simplicity of the pose, and the sombre colouring create a demure and deeply contemplative mood. It is interesting as an example of what can be done in profile portraiture. Nowadays the preference is for full or half-face studies, but the simplification of profile treatment has its advantages. It has an admirable directness of state-ment, and in the hands of a skilful artist lends itself to a very forcible delineation of character.

PLATE 20.—PORTRAIT OF A MAN: Boltraffio.

PLATE 21.—ANDREA MANTEGNA (1431–1506)
SCHOOL OF PADUA

" THE AGONY IN THE GARDEN "

PADUA, the seat of a famous university, was for a time the centre of a school of artists inspired, like the Florentines, with an intellectual fervour which made their work an important influence, especially on the beginnings of Venetian art. Of the Paduans, Mantegna was the greatest. With him must be considered the Bellinis, Jacopo and his two sons, Gentile and Giovanni. For a number of years they were resident in Padua, and Mantegna was married to a daughter of Jacopo. The influence of his father-in-law can be traced in Mantegna's art. Jacopo had a passion for painting religious pictures in which the actual subject was often overshadowed by its surroundings—fields and gardens, people coming and going, cities perched on precipitous rocks, all treated with a minute and vivid realism.

The effect of this style can be seen in " The Agony in the Garden." But Mantegna succeeded in imposing a unity of design and feeling upon his compositions which the older painter never achieved.

This is a strange picture, built up in startling pyramidal forms. The figure of Christ is at the apex of one of these, the eye being led upwards to where He kneels in isolation, by the rugged steps and the slope of the rocky hill as it rises from the stream. The same violent rhythm piles crag upon crag over this apocalyptic Jerusalem. The sinuous curves of the river serve by contrast to reinforce the boldness of the main design.

Headed by Judas, a troop of soldiers are coming from the town. Rabbits are playing on the roadway, and a cormorant is perched on the leafless tree. In the foreground the three disciples are sunk in a profound slumber. Angels bearing the instruments of the Passion descend from the sky, ominous with impending tragedy.

Mantegna was much influenced by Donatello. (He has placed his bronze statue of Gattamelata, which had just been erected at Padua, on the column seen against the highest tower of the city.) From him he derived a sculpturesque vision. This picture seems to be hewn out of stone. Everything is sharply cut and defined ; the colour is impressive and masterful. The whole work is informed with an austerity in keeping with its subject.

Such a severity of style, however, has its limitations. Mantegna's world is somewhat harsh and arid, too logic-ridden. It is remote from humanity, but it has its own commanding strength. That was his greatest gift to posterity.

PLATE 21.—THE AGONY IN THE GARDEN: Mantegna.

PLATE 22.—GIOVANNI BELLINI (1428?–1516)
SCHOOL OF PADUA

"THE AGONY IN THE GARDEN"

A GLANCE is sufficient to reveal the likeness which exists between this picture and Mantegna's. Both works are typically Paduan, both are articulated in the sculpturesque manner, born of an admiration for Donatello. The important point for us, however, is not the similarity of the two, but rather to notice wherein they diverge. For there are differences in the handling of the scene which point to the directions along which these two contemporaries were to develop.

In some respects Bellini's version is the less mature. The drawing is not so incisive. The figures of the disciples, for example, are less convincing. There is something rather desultory about their grouping, and one feels they would have had much ado to sleep in such attitudes. The angel appearing out of the sky with the Cup of the Passion is a rather feeble invention, and much more a *deus ex machina* than is Mantegna's apparition.

It is in the treatment of the landscape that the two pictures differ most widely. Instead of Mantegna's violent background carrying his sculpturesque formality to a severe and monumental climax, we look out over a wide valley, giving on to a plain that stretches between the gentle dip of the hills, to a sky suffused with daybreak. It is infinitely softer. The eye that almost recoils from Mantegna's rocky pinnacles is here lured to a distance where it can repose. The hill on the left is interesting. The grey escarpment of the quarry is a concession to the sterner mannerism, but it is mantled in green, and the buildings on the top are bathed in a clear light. In actuality this would be impossible, for the dawn is breaking from behind the hill; but one does not question it. It is sufficient that it produces its intended pleasurable effect.

Giovanni in this picture has created a strange and moving sympathy between the landscape and the scene of which it is the serene and silent witness. It is one of his contributions to art.

This is an early work, but it already reveals his sensitivity and depth of mood. We shall come back to him again, to find him a master of the school of Venetian portraiture.

PLATE 22.—THE AGONY IN THE GARDEN: Giovanni Bellini.

PLATE 23.—CARLO CRIVELLI (1430?–1493?)
VENETIAN SCHOOL

"THE ANNUNCIATION"

THE art of Venice, as one might expect, was complex in its origins. Padua, we have noted, had a strong influence upon the earlier Venetian painters. Crivelli, one of the most talented of these, does not, however, at first sight, appear to owe much to that school of precise logicians. What strikes one immediately about his pictures is his love of ornament, a trait that quite obviously must be attributed to a different source.

He received his training at the island of Murano, where a flourishing school of workers in mosaic and glass kept alive the Byzantine predilection for costly and elaborate decoration. From the very first his art suggests the practice of the goldsmith. He delights in covering the surfaces of his pictures with a profusion of detail almost jewel-like in its brilliance.

"The Annunciation" reveals very clearly his love of splendour. Other qualities, however, disengage themselves. The architectural forms are treated with a strict attention to perspective, and have a clear-cut solidity such as the Paduans would have approved. This picture is at once ornate and severe.

Through a doorway flanked with richly carved pilasters the Madonna is seen at prayer. A ray of golden light descends upon her, passing through the wall of the palace in its course. Outside, the Archangel halts, kneeling, his hand uplifted in salutation. He bears a lily, the symbol of the Virgin's purity. At his side is St. Emidius, the patron saint of Ascoli (for which town this picture was executed). He is holding a model of that city in his hand and seems to be taking a lively interest in what is happening. Not so, however, are the gentlemen at the top of the steps on the left, and the very charming and human figure of the little girl peeping round the balustrade. The upper storey of the palace is richly embellished. The inlaid ceiling, the dove and peacock, the carpet hanging down from the loggia, all attest Crivelli's insatiable love of profusion.

Magnificence was to be a recurrent note in Venetian painting, and with Crivelli it has begun.

The ideals which he pursued are not those of our own age in art. In our desire for clear statement of form we are content to sacrifice detail in painting, as in architecture, and many of us will feel unmoved by Crivelli's rather pedantic synthesis of elaboration and severity.

PLATE 23.—THE ANNUNCIATION: Crivelli.

PLATE 24.—ANTONELLO DA MESSINA (1444–1493)
VENETIAN SCHOOL

"PORTRAIT OF A YOUNG MAN"

ANTONELLO DA MESSINA was destined to play an important part in the development of Venetian art. He came to Venice from Sicily, and with him brought a knowledge that gave him a unique distinction among his contemporaries. He had mastered the technique of oil-painting, and more than that, he had acquired the method of handling the medium which was employed by the early Flemish painters, Van Eyck in particular. Vasari says that this was the result of an actual journey to the Netherlands, but it is much more likely that he had come in contact with Flemish artists then working at the Court of Naples, and adopted their procedure.

This consisted in superimposing glazes of transparent oil-colouring on a ground begun in tempera. The firm drawing and precision of the older medium was retained, and to it was added a subtlety of tone and luminosity which opened the way to countless new effects. Greater breadth of handling, a fluency of colour, more realistic lighting, followed in consequence, and these were exactly the qualities most eagerly sought after by the rising generation of painters.

This " Portrait of a Young Man " (supposed to be the artist himself) shows him in full possession of these powers. The head is firmly drawn, its contours being realized with an impressive solidity that nowhere is over-weighted. The shadows on the cheek-bone and under the chin give a high relief that was not attempted by Botticelli in his portrait study (Plate 9). The effect is one of an increased realism. The slightly sardonic expression of the eyes and mouth is admirably realized. The colour scheme is simple and effective.

While Antonello contributed greatly to Venice, he in turn learnt much from the Venetians. His little masterpiece, " The Crucifixion," in the National Gallery, reveals the influence of Giovanni Bellini. The wide and serene landscape is full of a sympathetic intensity which makes this work one of the tenderest and most moving Crucifixions ever painted.

Interesting in another way is his " St. Jerome in his Study." There the clear transparency of the painting, the felicity of the lighting, the minute delineation of detail, have caused this picture to be mistaken for the work of Van Eyck himself. It is not surprising that an artist of such consummate skill, especially in his handling of the coming medium of oils, should have left his mark indelibly on the development of later art.

PLATE 24.—PORTRAIT OF A YOUNG MAN: Antonello.

PLATE 25.—GIOVANNI BELLINI (1428?–1516)
VENETIAN SCHOOL

"PORTRAIT OF THE DOGE LOREDANO"

GIOVANNI BELLINI returned to Venice with his family sometime about 1460. His early "Agony in the Garden" had been painted in Padua. Henceforth Venice was to be the scene of his labours. His work rapidly increased in power and sensitivity. Religious subjects continued to occupy him, and these, like our beautiful "Madonna of the Meadow," illustrate his growing command of colour, and his ability to create a subtle spiritual affinity between his subjects and the landscapes with which he surrounded them.

Meanwhile his brother Gentile was becoming one of the most memorable portrait painters of the time. This branch of art, in turn, claimed Giovanni's attention. He was commissioned to paint several state portraits of the Doges, and this work, executed about 1503, is justly regarded as one of his masterpieces.

Loredano was the seventy-fourth Doge of Venice, and his reign coincided with a stirring and important period of history. Henry VIII. of England was his contemporary, as was Francis I. of France. In Rome the Pontificates of Julius II. and Leo X. were eventful alike in affairs of Church and State, and the ruler of the most powerful and wealthy city in Italy held an office that was no sinecure.

We see him in this portrait, a man of sagacity and quiet strength, of justice tempered with clemency. His face is worn and ascetic, spiritualized by suffering, yet full of the repose of maturity and of the plenitude of life. Few portraits have the same power of riveting our attention and remaining in the mind's eye long afterwards, clear and precise, the symbol of a type as well as the likeness of an individual man.

The colouring is simple and striking, its dusky blue background contrasted with warm tones of salmon red and silvery greys.

Giovanni Bellini's work would be impressive for its own qualities. When we remember that Giorgione entered his studio as a boy of eleven, that the youthful Titian worked under him, and that a host of other painters, among them Palma Vecchio and Lorenzo Lotto, owed much to his example, we can hardly overestimate his influence on the course of Venetian painting.

PLATE 25.—PORTRAIT OF THE DOGE LOREDANO: Giovanni Bellini.

PLATE 26.—TITIAN (1489–1576)

VENETIAN SCHOOL

"THE HOLY FAMILY"

THE change that came over Venetian painting at the beginning of the sixteenth century owes its origin very largely to Giorgione. He was a singularly individualistic painter. The rarity of the works which can definitely be assigned to him, the romantic and elusive qualities which are the mark of his school, and his brief career cut short by his death at thirty-three, all contribute to the glamour which surrounds him. His contributions to art fall under two headings. As a technician he was an accomplished master of oil-painting, using that medium with a sensitivity and freedom which point the way to the great Venetian colourists. In his choice of subjects and in his handling of them a new spirit can be detected. Hitherto art had been to a great extent ceremonial. Its masterpieces had been created for public occasions, religious and civic. The vein of lyricism in Giorgione turned rather to an intimate subjectivity. He began the taste for genre pictures ; not the naturalistic genre painting we are accustomed to at a later age (Giorgione was a symbolist, not a realist), but scenes inspired by classical poetry, or drawn from contemporary life, heightened and idealized, and inclining more and more to the pursuits of music and love. This led to a liberation of manner. The severity of the earlier masters was forgotten. All must come now, as Yeats has put it, " to sight and touch," and the subtlety of the flesh enters at last into its own. It is necessary to remember this as we begin our study of his great contemporary.

Giorgione's death in 1510 left Titian the undisputed master of the Venetian School. As young men, they had worked together in Giovanni Bellini's studio, and our mysterious and beautiful picture, "The Golden Age," which Sir Charles Holmes claims as an early Titian, is distinctly Giorgionesque in feeling. Vasari says that at one period it is almost impossible to distinguish their two styles.

Titian's quality can be much better grasped from the two later works we have illustrated, but this " Holy Family," though it is the outcome of his apprenticeship, shows the direction in which his art was tending. There is a striving for a greater breadth of treatment, a more human-istic naturalism. The Madonna and Child bear the imprint of genius, and, although somewhat rough in execution, so does the vivid and lovely shepherd boy kneeling on the right. But Titian is not yet quite sure of himself, and we must regard this as a work of promise rather than of achievement.

PLATE 26.—THE HOLY FAMILY : Titian.

PLATE 27.—TITIAN (1489–1576)
VENETIAN SCHOOL

"ARIOSTO"

WE could do worse in our consideration of this picture than by beginning with the painting of the sleeve. It occupies so much of the canvas that we can have no doubt this was a deliberate intention of Titian's. The first thing that strikes one is the extreme sense of solidity, of mass, which it conveys. Titian, no less than the Florentines, was concerned with three dimensional representation. Looking closer, we are next aware that the fabric of the material, the voluminous almost quilted folds of grey silken stuff, has been realized with a masterly precision. Not only the form but the texture, the actual substance, has been set down. This was one of Titian's most notable contributions to painting.

The Florentines, especially the early masters, were content to work in a direct sculpturesque manner, so that their human beings seem carved out of stone. For subtlety of surface they had little use, and tempera-painting with its cool bright colours did not lend itself to this end.

The adding of a *substantial* reality to the already understood representation of volume and mass gave to painting a new power of stimulus. It became infinitely more sensuous, appealing almost to the sense of touch. We really *feel* as well as *see* the sleeve in this picture. A sort of transcendent materialism enters into art.

The delineation of the face is masterful. The wide forehead, the dark solemnity of the hair, the sensitive and proud expression, are full of that plenitude of being wherein flesh and soul are one. Neither takes precedence, both being poised, as it were, in a complete and perfect balance.

The colour is rich and subdued, its harmonies of greys and silver and glowing jet all contributing to the profound inner mood of this picture. It is the earliest portrait of Titian's that we possess, but it already reveals him as a supreme master.

PLATE 27.—ARIOSTO: Titian.

PLATE 28.—TITIAN (1489–1576)
VENETIAN SCHOOL

"BACCHUS AND ARIADNE"

WITH this amazing work we pass into that world of joyous paganism that gave so many subjects to Titian in the middle period of his art. It is one of the gallery's most treasured possessions. Poussin learnt much from it, and our own painters of the eighteenth century were indebted to it in their pursuit of the grand manner.

Ariadne, the daughter of Minos, has been deserted by Theseus, and is here seen surprised by the youthful Bacchus and his train of nymphs and fauns and satyrs.

It is a complex work. One may compare it to a symphony in which successive movements are contrasted, successive melodic and harmonic matter developed with virtuosity, the whole being knit together by an unerring grasp of the principles that make for unity. The picture is full of movement. It begins with the Bacchanalian revelry sweeping into the canvas from the right. The figure of Ariadne, also in vigorous action, reverses, as it were, the direction of the motion, turning it back upon itself. But in the centre of the picture an interesting thing happens. The movement is arrested. It is brought to a halt in the two stationary leopards. Even the powerful vertical of the right leg of Bacchus as he springs from his car helps to establish a break in the horizontal surge of the Bacchanals. He, as befits the central personage, is a pivot round which rhythm and counter-rhythm swing. The little faun in the foreground adds to this effect. In him the speed of motion is slowed down and comes to a halt, emphasized by the dog who faces its onset, and by the drapery and urn lying on the ground.

Equally impressive is the handling of the colour — the warm, glowing flesh tints, so typical of the mature Titian, the luminous blues and reds. The landscape (not very adequately reproduced in this plate) is marvellous in its depth of gentian and amethyst. The painting of the crown of ivy leaves on the head of Bacchus has long been famous; but indeed everywhere Titian has been lavish of his gifts. The eye can return to this picture again and again without coming to the end of its discoveries. It is one of the most amazing pictorial compositions in existence.

PLATE 28.—BACCHUS AND ARIADNE : Titian.

PLATE 29.—PALMA VECCHIO (1480–1528)
VENETIAN SCHOOL

"PORTRAIT OF A POET"

THIS portrait has much in common with the "Ariosto" of Titian, at which we have been looking. It has been ascribed to Titian, but is now generally accepted as the work of Palma, his contemporary. He was one of that distinguished group of painters who issued from the studio of Bellini.

This quiet and thoughtful painting is an example of the romantic type of portraiture inaugurated by Giorgione. The face resembles that of Ariosto, but in this, as indeed in the Titian portrait, we are not quite certain as to the identity of the sitter.

It has been said that whereas the Florentines expressed themselves in line, the Venetians did so in colour, and Vasari—a partisan in this connection—goes so far as to say that the Venetians used colour to cover up an inadequacy of draughtsmanship. This is not so, but it reveals how an eye, accustomed to the succinct precision of tempera, may have reacted to the new and sensuous harmonies of oil-painting.

Especially noteworthy is the painting of the white linen collar and the glowing crimson of the voluminous sleeves. There is something slightly effeminate in the mildness of the face, and this feeling is increased by the delicate five-strand necklace of gold the poet is wearing. The dark background bears sprays of the wild olive, sacred to the Muses.

It is a glowing and restful piece of work, with a languorous charm of its own, but there is a lack of the incisive vitality we should expect if we were to credit its assignation to Titian.

PLATE 29.—PORTRAIT OF A POET: Palma Vecchio.

PLATE 30.—MORETTO (1498–1555)
SCHOOL OF BRESCIA

"PORTRAIT OF AN ITALIAN NOBLEMAN"

MORETTO was born in Brescia about 1498. That city during the first half of the sixteenth century was the home of a group of artists closely allied to the Venetians. It is not known whether Moretto ever visited Venice, but he must have come under the influence of Titian, as this picture bears a definite likeness to his style.

The love of painting fabrics is at once apparent, the various textures being rendered with a sensuous skill. Notice the painting of the rich ermine stole, of the green silken sleeves, and of the elaborately patterned curtain hanging in the background. There is a silvery iridescence in the colour (very strikingly seen in the original of this picture), and this quality is one for which the Brescians are famed.

The young nobleman is wearing a plumed head-dress, and inscribed on an ornament on the brim is a motto in Greek lettering which reads : " Alas ! I desire Julia." Based on this, conjectures have been made as to the identity of the sitter, but for us it is enough to notice the love-sick air so admirably portrayed. He is an exquisitely languid young man, fond of fine clothes and delicate living.

There is, perhaps, a certain lack of vitality in this picture, a feeling of decadence, not without a hint of fatigue, of surfeit even. Moroni, the other notable Brescian, if somewhat narrower in his outlook, was more of a realist, as one can see from his " Portrait of a Tailor," also in the gallery.

Moretto painted many altar-pieces which reveal his command of silvery colouring. For all its listlessness, this portrait is not unworthy to take its place among the great Venetians of his time. That in itself is no small praise.

PLATE 30.—PORTRAIT OF AN ITALIAN NOBLEMAN: Moretto.

PLATE 31.—LORENZO LOTTO (1480-1556)
VENETIAN SCHOOL

" LUCREZIA "

GREATER than either Palma Vecchio or Moretto, but not so great as Titian, Lorenzo Lotto is a painter who has suffered not a little undue neglect. He is not perhaps strikingly original, but his craftsmanship is of a singularly high order, and he had the Venetian command of rich and sumptuous colour.

This " Lucrezia," acquired for the gallery on the recent break-up of the collection at Dorchester House, is an excellent example of his work. The title is somewhat fortuitous, for it is derived from the drawing which the lady holds in her hands depicting the Roman Lucrezia about to plunge a dagger in her breast. The comely and decidedly substantial Venetian dame is not likely to resort to such extremes. She is much too comfortable, too well upholstered both in her person and her attire, to be a subject for hysteria.

Lotto has invested her with a voluminous femininity. Her dress is beautifully painted, its rich red-orange contrasted with the sheen of dark green satin. The flesh tints are pure and transparent. Her face shows her to be fully conscious of the charm offered by its regular features, a charm that is amply supported by the generosity of her bust.

Her head-dress is interesting, a wig of curled wool tied with silken bows.

One does not feel that her slightly dramatic gesture, possibly one of protest, has any very deep significance, still less points to any moral.

Lotto uses the subject as an excuse for a rich and harmonious colour composition, thoroughly Venetian in its opulence and its sensitivity to tactile values.

PLATE 31.—LUCREZIA: Lorenzo Lotto.

PLATE 32.—PAOLO VERONESE (1528–1588)
VENETIAN SCHOOL

" ST. HELENA : VISION OF THE INVENTION OF THE CROSS "

VERONESE brings us to another aspect of Venetian art. It was an age of magnificence, and large decorative paintings for the walls and ceilings of the palaces were in much demand. Veronese was a supreme master of decoration. His most famous work is probably the immense " Marriage Feast at Cana " which is in the Louvre. No one else would have attempted such a task. Our own fine work, " The Family of Darius before Alexander," is full of the splendour of pageantry. These vast canvases, so crowded with incident, have such a fundamental soundness of design, very often quite geometrical in its conception, that they are never diffuse. Their energy is concentrated, and the effect is one of balance and repose. The subtlety of Veronese's colour, his silvery blues and pinks, the sheen of his textures, and his quiet and unobtrusive lighting, all contribute to this unity.

The " St. Helena with her Vision of the Invention of the Cross," though it is surpassed by several other of his works in the National Gallery, gives us a very good insight into Veronese's quality. It has frequently been pointed out how its design is built up out of a number of strong diagonals contrasted with horizontal lines, forming a series of triangular and diamond-shaped units subtly related to each other.

The colouring is very typical. It is warm and glowing, passages of rich pink and of luminous saffrons in St. Helena's dress contrasted with the darker tones, and the shadowy wings of the angels bearing the Cross hovering against a sky of pale golden light. In the original these subtle harmonies of old rose and gold are suffused with a silvery radiance. It is difficult to describe his method. He keeps his shadows full of vivid colour and touches his high lights with streaks of brilliant impasto, sometimes using touches of pure white. The result is the miraculous sheen which glitters from his canvases.

He is not concerned, like Michelangelo, for example, with any profound spiritual significance—he is more purely a painter ; but in the handling of large passages of colour, in the manipulation of broad decorative design, he is unsurpassed.

PLATE 32.—ST. HELENA. VISION OF THE INVENTION OF THE CROSS:
Veronese.

PLATE 33.—TINTORETTO (1518–1594)
VENETIAN SCHOOL

" ST. GEORGE AND THE DRAGON "

TINTORETTO, like so many Italian painters, is known to us by his nickname. He was christened Jacopo, the son of Battista Robusti, cloth and silk dyer (*tintore*) of Venice. Hence his appellation, " The Little Dyer." The name suggests colour. Romantic biographers could easily find for his childhood a romantic environment. The lagoons, the ochre-pink façades of palaces, the glowing mosaics of St. Mark—these he shared with his contemporaries—never to mention the rich dyes of his father's shop. For him with lavish kindness the gifts of God were strown. And then Titian for his master ! So the story begins, and because he was a promising youth with an infinite capacity for hard work, the end was what one might expect. He became one of the greatest colourists in the history of Italian art.

Our " St. George and the Dragon " is one of his finest works. It is full of an amazing vigour. The charge of the Saint, his long spear thrust at the monster, the flying princess in the foreground, and the scurry of wild clouds in the sky—these at once are obvious. Taken separately they are what any imaginative illustrator might have conjured up. But the secret of this picture lies in the way in which Tintoretto has fused these episodes into a magical whole.

His colour has much to do with this. The prevailing tone is a silvery green contrasted with splendours of luminous pink and blue. The design achieves its effect by a repetition of *motif*, the eye being subtly led from one focus of action to another—the whirlwind of the princess's robes, the vertigo of the conflict with the dragon, and the dramatic maelstrom of the sky. A ground is given for these by the singular landscape. From the dark foreground with its distorted tree-trunk, we follow the indented seashore to the straining wood and the hoary castle walls. Hoary is the right word, for here is the beginning of that romantic treatment of nature that was to suggest many a reverie to Claude and Turner, and furnish that view from Keats's " Magic casements " and the setting for Tennyson's " Blow, bugles, blow."

With this picture the invasion of fairyland had begun.

PLATE 33.—ST. GEORGE AND THE DRAGON: Tintoretto.

PLATE 34.—TINTORETTO (1518-1594)
VENETIAN SCHOOL

"THE ORIGIN OF THE MILKY WAY"

THE story goes that Titian, seeing how well the boy could draw, dismissed Tintoretto somewhat unceremoniously from his studio. But the youth would have appeared to have harboured no ill will, for he set up as a motto on his own walls, "The design of Michelangelo and the colouring of Titian." It was a high standard, and this beautiful work shows that he did not fall far short of his ambition.

Jupiter, coming down from Olympus, attended by his eagle, is in the act of snatching the infant Hercules from the breast of his mother, Juno. The startled goddess, surrounded by her *amorini* and her glowing peacocks, makes a vain attempt at resistance, while " the lacteal jets from her breasts " (this is a quotation) " burst forth into the constellation known as the Milky Way." That is the legend which Tintoretto has translated into a superb piece of pictorial rhetoric.

The violent foreshortened figure of Jupiter might have come from the hand of Michelangelo. The audacity of its swinging motion is at once apparent. Sweeping up from the right of the picture comes another rhythm, undulating like a wave, bearing upon it the peacocks, the recumbent Cupid, and the rich draperies of Juno's couch.

Half-reclining, half-floating on its crest, the radiant goddess is poised in a perilous equilibrium. Her body is one of the loveliest nudes in existence. Round it pivots all the swinging motion of this picture, for by a miracle of spatial handling its violence is checked, held in balance at the centre of the action. Notice how the Cupid, flying towards her right arm, helps to support the composition by reversing the momentum of the other figures.

A rich crimson canopy fills the top left-hand corner, while below, yet another of the *amorini* is buoyed upwards on a fuliginous cloud, spangled with the first drops of the constellation.

The passages of colour are indescribably beautiful. The painting of the peacocks has long been famous. It is only one of many similar felicities.

Tintoretto was the last of the Venetian giants. In this picture we are able to see him in the plenitude of his power.

PLATE 34.—THE ORIGIN OF THE MILKY WAY : Tintoretto.

PLATE 35.—FRANCESCO GUARDI (1712-1793)
VENETIAN SCHOOL

"VIEW IN VENICE"

AFTER Titian and Tintoretto and Veronese the art of Venice suffered a decline. For a hundred years nothing of first-rate importance was produced, but at the opening of the eighteenth century Tiepolo began what was really the swan-song of Venetian art. He was a superb decorator with a brilliant command of colour, and could fling across a ceiling a rout of elegant figures in every possible attitude. Our collection possesses one or two small easel pictures from his hand, but nothing so imposing as his magnificent "Finding of Moses" which is one of the glories of the Scottish National Gallery.

Canaletto, an architectural painter, was his contemporary. His transparent objective style won him many admirers, and excellent specimens of his work may be seen at Trafalgar Square. With him can be included Guardi, whose "View of Venice" is illustrated on the opposite page. It has not the limpid lucidity of Canaletto, but shows the same preference for architectural compositions.

In the foreground numerous figures in the attire of the period are seen on the flagged piazetta. To the left is a church tower, and in the centre the arch of a bridge unites the two blocks of buildings. It is a pleasant picture, full of exact observation, but that is about all one can say.

Nothing lasts for ever. Italy, so long the mother of the arts, reached a point of exhaustion. It was only to be expected. No other country ever produced such a lineage of great masters. In doing so she spent herself so prodigally that the barren season was bound to come. Our next section takes us away from the Mediterranean and the Adriatic to a very different scene, to the wealthy mercantile cities of the Nether-lands. And as we come north we shall have to retrace our steps in time, in order to see the beginnings of an art that after that of Italy was as prolific as any other, and with the exception of the French, has given as much to the inheritance of Europe.

PLATE 35.—VIEW IN VENICE : Guardi.

PLATE 36.—JAN VAN EYCK (1385?–1441)
EARLY FLEMISH SCHOOL

"JAN ARNOLFINI AND HIS WIFE"

THIS strange and arresting picture is one of the most remarkable in the annals of art. The history of painting is full of many surprises, of unforeseen and unaccountable manifestations of genius, but it is safe to say that the case of the Van Eycks (for with Jan Eyck must be included his elder brother Hubert) is without a parallel. They were the fathers of the Flemish School. As such, one might expect them to be primitives, breaking new ground with experimental *naïveté* and hesitation, artists of promise rather than of fulfilment. Instead we are confronted with work that reveals a consummate mastery.

It is impossible in the limited space at our disposal to give any adequate analysis of this work. In the first place, we shall have to state merely in passing that the Van Eycks may be said to have invented the craft of oil-painting. Their purely technical discoveries in this field alone would have made them memorable.

Jan painted this picture at Bruges in the year 1434. He has signed it, in a passage of exquisite calligraphy, on the wall above the mirror, "Johannes de Eyck fuit hic (was here) 1434." In Italy, Fra Angelico was still painting his hieratic masterpieces in pure and flat colouring. Here we have already the subtlety of naturalistic lighting, and of minute and vivid realism. Uccello was puzzling out the problems of linear perspective. Van Eyck has solved them through sheer observation. The representation of solid forms was still being pursued by the Italians in the monumental and geometrical manner of Masaccio and Piero della Francesca. Van Eyck achieves it at once by what seems to be a purely instinctive insight.

The design of this picture is at once simple and impressive. The two upright figures divide the composition almost equally. The vertical effect is emphasized by the lines of the window, of the pendent chandelier, and the crimson bed-hangings. But any feeling of stiffness is dissipated by the extraordinary variety of incidental forms Van Eyck has introduced into the picture. The eye at once fixes upon the convex mirror, upon whose painting he has lavished a microscopic virtuosity. Indeed, all the details are fascinating—the curiously shaped slippers lying on the floor, the sprightly little terrier, the vivid serpentine twists of the white border on the lady's skirt, the clustered ruching hanging from her wide fur-trimmed sleeve, the oranges under the window, and even the leaves and fruit of the cherry tree outside.

To Van Eyck's depth of feeling and power of characterization we shall have to refer again.

36

PLATE 36.—JAN ARNOLFINI AND HIS WIFE: Jan Van Eyck.

PLATE 37.—JAN VAN EYCK (1385?–1441)
EARLY FLEMISH SCHOOL

" A MAN'S PORTRAIT "

WE were so preoccupied with the detail of our last picture that we had not space to note the subtle human interest it contains. Jan Van Eyck could sum up very incisively the personality of the people he painted. Arnolfini has not escaped his acute observation. A rather grim and cold and puritanical specimen, we feel that we know as much about him as we know of a character in a novel by Balzac or Dostoievsky. And the same is true of his timid and younger and exquisitely modest wife. Their intimate yet very decorous relationship is expressed in the grave and almost ceremonious way in which their hands are joined.

His power of analysis is revealed strikingly in this portrait. The face is shrewd and wily, that of a just and hard man reaping, one would suspect, where he had not sown, and gathering where he had not strawed. Van Eyck has not spared him. There is a ruthless quality in his penetration. Every wrinkle, every revealing line, is set down with exactness—the cold eyes, the narrow lips, the firm cheek bones and chin. It is, indeed, almost too photographic, and the smooth surface finish of his paint, the result of complicated processes of glazing with films of transparent colour, adds to the realistic effect. As though he were conscious of this acid and somewhat over-deliberate manner, Van Eyck has let himself go in his flowing treatment of the highly flamboyant head-dress. It is painted with a rich and emphatic flourish. Its glowing passage of colour supplies the decorative note that was needed to give this rather severe study its æsthetic quality.

Van Eyck, like Rubens, lived a life of affairs that brought him into a close and vivid contact with his fellow-men. He was attached to the court of Philip the Good, Duke of Burgundy, and had travelled widely. One can imagine that, quite apart from his qualities as a painter, his almost alarming powers of insight into human nature commended him highly to a prince of the time.

The example of Van Eyck, with his consummate technique in the handling of oil paint, his acute sense of detail and psychological penetration, set a high standard for subsequent painters. On the frame of this picture he has inscribed the motto, " Als ich can." It is part of a Flemish proverb, " As I can, not as I will," and has been taken as a proof of the artist's humility. Sir Charles Holmes, however, makes the interesting comment that, " since five centuries of effort and ambition have failed to rival such accomplishment, we may be pardoned for wondering if the words were not also a sly challenge."

PLATE 37.—A MAN'S PORTRAIT: Jan Van Eyck.

PLATE 38—ROBERT CAMPIN (1375-1444)
EARLY FLEMISH SCHOOL

"PORTRAITS OF A MAN AND HIS WIFE"

THE ascription of these two portraits has for long been a matter of conjecture. By more or less unanimous consent they were assigned to the Maître de Flémalle, the inheritor of the Van Eyck tradition in early Flemish art, but his identity remained a subject of dispute. One Jacques Daret, fellow artist of the more famous Roger van der Weyden, was suggested as the likely master, but the most recent research has identified the Maître de Flémalle as Robert Campin, and to Robert Campin we are fairly safe in attributing these works.

He was born about 1375, and thus was actually older than Jan Van Eyck, but little is known of him until some thirty years later, when we find him settled as a painter at Tournai.

A glance at these portraits shows that he had mastered the Van Eycks' technique, in all probability through having worked under Hubert at some time. The portrait of the man bears a distinct resemblance, especially in the head-dress, to the **Jan Van Eyck** portrait at which we have been looking.

Again the most prominent note is one of a vigorous realism and power of characterization. The expression on the man's face is decidedly severe and forbidding, and it is with pleasure that we turn to the plump and more genial features of his wife. She is almost peasant-like in her fresh engaging simplicity.

There is little spiritual quality in either of the portraits. They are sharp and exact, lacking in the graciousness that would have crept somehow or other into an Italian painter's vision. The linen head-dress of the wife is, however, beautifully painted, and invests the picture with its cool and voluminous charm.

Campin's importance is increased by the fact that he had for pupils Roger van der Weyden, and in all probability Dirk Bouts, who is the painter of the Madonna and Child illustrated in our next plate.

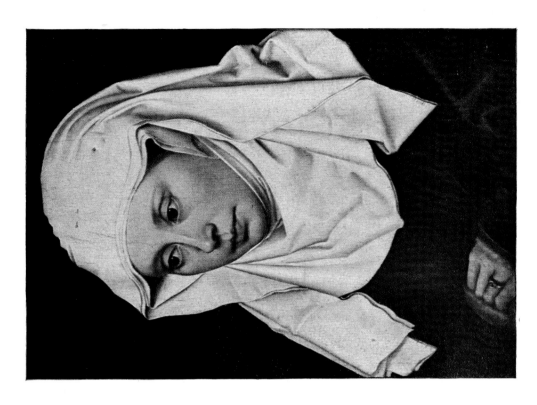

PLATE 38.—PORTRAITS OF A MAN AND HIS WIFE : Early Flemish School.

PLATE 39.—DIRK BOUTS (1400–1475)
EARLY FLEMISH SCHOOL

" MADONNA AND CHILD ENTHRONED "

DIRK BOUTS was born at Haarlem in 1400. Little is known of his early life, but the similarity of his style with Robert Campin, especially noticeable in his " Virgin and Child " (2595 in the National Gallery), would point to the fact that he had studied under that master at Tournai. He came south, and settled in Louvain about 1440.

His " Entombment " (664) is one of his most interesting works. It is painted in tempera upon linen, a method then in vogue for religious banners ; and although such a process has not the permanency of oil colours used on a carefully prepared canvas, it is in a wonderful state of preservation. The figures round the dead body of Christ are grouped with a compactness and strength of cohesion that is frequently absent in his work, and the picture is memorable for the green and airy landscape in the background. Bouts, like Perugino who was to come after him, had a feeling for the sympathetic treatment of gentle and luminous landscape.

This " Madonna and Child Enthroned " possesses one little passage of such, seen through the Gothic archway on the left. It is interesting to note that he has discovered (as Perugino was to discover) how a slender and feathery tree can be used to give a sense of distance and space. For the rest, this rather dry and formal picture conforms to the Gothic altarpiece of the time. The Madonna sits on a canopied throne, between St. Peter, holding a gospel book, and St. Paul, who is offering a flower to the Infant Christ.

These figures have an undoubted solidity. It is sculpturesque in its own way, though not in the superb marmoreal manner of the Italians. Rather, one detects a resemblance in style to the craft of wood-carving, practised so extensively by Gothic sculptors. The folds of the crimson mantle of the Virgin suggest unmistakably the wood-carver's art. They seem cut out rather than modelled—a slight distinction perhaps, but one which is noticeable again and again whenever Flemish art approaches the sculpturesque.

There is a lack of ecstasy in this picture, a certain muddiness of colour, which the sombre tones of St. Peter's attire, and the dull browns of the brocade panel behind the Virgin, do nothing to dispel. Our next illustration—possibly a little out of sequence here, but, since it belongs to Northern as opposed to Mediterranean art, better included among these Gothic religious panels—calls us back to the vivid singing power of pure colour.

PLATE 39.—MADONNA AND CHILD ENTHRONED: Early Flemish School.

PLATE 40.—ARTIST UNKNOWN (14TH CENTURY)
EARLY ENGLISH (OR FRENCH ?) SCHOOL

"THE WILTON DIPTYCH"

THIS very lovely work is one of the most interesting of recent additions to the gallery. It was formerly in the possession of the Earl of Pembroke at Wilton House, whence it derives its name. There has been much discussion as to its source, but in the space at our disposal it will be better to give some description of the work, and point out certain features which relate it to the art of the period, even though they leave its origin a matter of conjecture.

We know that it was painted for Richard II. some time about the year 1380. The young king is seen kneeling in the left-hand panel, and with him are represented St. Edmund, St. Edward the Confessor, and St. John the Baptist. Round his neck is a collar of broom pods (*plantagenista*), in allusion to his dynasty, and the exquisite cope-shaped robe that he is wearing bears his device of a hart, embroidered in golden thread. In the right-hand panel the Virgin is holding the Infant Saviour in her arms. His hand is extended in blessing. An angel supports a pennant with a red cross, and the rest of the panel is filled with angels wearing wreaths of roses. Their pointed wings make a most beautiful pattern against the richly gilded background. The intensity of the blue is quite indescribable. The whole work is informed with a sense of glory, and quite clearly has been designed and painted by an artist who is a master at his craft.

As to its position in art, certain facts are beyond dispute. It is Gothic in style, and has much in common with the exquisite work of the illuminators of the period. In France this art reached its highest perfection, and those who have seen French work of the late mediæval period will recognize an immediate identity of style. Hence it has frequently been credited to the French School. But the fact remains that it was executed in England for an English king, and that we possess in the life-size portrait of Richard II. in Westminster Abbey another work which, despite its difference in scale, suggests that it might be the work of the same artist. It is not unreasonable to suppose that he was an Englishman, and the brilliant school of illuminators which flourished in this country about the year 1400 justifies the belief that there were native artists quite capable of producing such a delightful work. Its acquisition by the gallery was an event of national importance. Its loveliness is beyond dispute, and we cannot be too thankful for the chance which spared this diptych from the vandalism that destroyed nearly all the English panel-paintings of that time.

40

PLATE 40.—THE WILTON DIPTYCH: Early English (or French ?) School.

PLATE 41.—HANS MEMLING (1430?–1494)
EARLY FLEMISH SCHOOL

"THE VIRGIN AND THE INFANT CHRIST"

MEMLING has always been one of the most popular of the early Flemish painters. He has been called the Fra Angelico of the North, but like most superficial comparisons the epithet hardly holds good. For it is better to admit that Flemish religious art never reached the heights of the early Italians. It remains much more earthly. The Van Eycks' " Adoration of the Lamb " has indeed much of the heavenly vision, but even of it one critic writes, " The angels sing conscientiously enough, but they are not spirits, nor is their song of flaming fire." That quality of transport is not to be found in Flemish art, which is essentially realistic. Such spirituality it possesses is of a much more mundane order. It does not knock at the gates of the unseen. The religious genius of the North found its most complete expression in the Gothic cathedral, not in painting.

But when that is said, how much is left that is charming. Hans Memling, whose name suggests a German extraction, lived and painted in Bruges when that city was at the height of her fame. As ever, altarpieces were in much demand. They postulated a rather conventional composition, the stage being set as it were ; in the centre, the Virgin upon her canopied throne, attended by such figures as the artist or his patron wished to introduce. Not that that in any sense precluded a highly personal approach to the work. But the theme of the Madonna and Child, which gave to the Italians the occasion of many of their most superb and original inspirations, does not seem to have evoked the same response in their Flemish contemporaries. Seldom, if ever, do we escape from the rather precise formularies of the miniature painters. Pictures such as this Memling are in reality miniatures on a larger scale, or indeed a series of miniatures on the same panel. Their charm arises from their vivid and imaginative handling of detail rather than in any dominating spiritual passion. How exquisite this can be one sees from the estuary in the background, with its ship in full sail setting out on some strange romantic voyage ; or in the painting of the armour of St. George, with its high lights of steely blue ; or in the portraiture of the donor, who kneels in an attitude of prayer. The Virgin is mild and bland. Like Botticelli's Madonnas she is not profoundly interested in her rôle, but on the other hand she is very obviously there, not far away in a world that is distractingly sweet and sad.

This picture has a tender quality, the happiness of pleasing incidents invested with a rich yet never over-stimulating colour. As such, it is a very complete expression of Memling's art.

PLATE 41.—THE VIRGIN AND INFANT CHRIST: Memling.

Plate 42.—GERARD DAVID (1460-1523)

EARLY FLEMISH SCHOOL

"THE MYSTIC MARRIAGE OF ST. CATHERINE"

GERARD DAVID, one of the most famous followers of Memling, was, like so many Flemish painters, born in Holland. He came south to the wealthier country and settled in Bruges, and although there are traces of Dutch mannerism, especially in his earlier work, his art in the main was formed by the city of his adoption.

In the Flanders of the fifteenth century it was impossible to be an artist at all and not to be an adept at the handling of oil paint in the way inaugurated by the Van Eycks. Perhaps, indeed, we may regret that the Flemish School sprang into such technical competence at its very outset. After the Van Eycks, what advance was possible? Towards what greater perfection could one aspire? The currents of life moved in the same familiar channels. Religious paintings and realistic portraiture became a daily round, if far removed indeed from a trivial task. For the Flemish, unlike the Florentines, were not theorists. They were never carried away on the wings of speculation. The insatiable intellectual activity of a Leonardo or a Michelangelo never troubled their work with its excitement and passion. And so their art, after the surprising achievement of the Van Eycks, remains comparatively static. This is not, however, to suggest that their accomplishment was anything other than immense.

Look at this "Mystic Marriage of St. Catherine" and compare it with the Dirk Bouts and Memling pictures just illustrated. Allowing for the inevitable slight differences in colouring and handling, the impression is one of a rather monotonous similarity. Then think for a moment of the highly distinctive personal styles of, say, Botticelli and Ghirlandaio and Leonardo. It is possibly an unfair comparison, but the fact remains that the variation of these pictures is one of detail rather than of general effect, just as it is in the realization of detail one finds their most compelling charm.

This is, indeed, the work of a master. The impressive solidity of the demure personages assisting at the rite (the Infant Christ is placing a marriage ring upon the extended finger of St. Catherine), the ease of the handling, the cool greys and dark greens of the airy architectural setting, the vivid treatment of the infinitely intricate and minute, as in the fabrics and jewellery work, all proclaim it to be such. Is it unkind, perhaps, to remember that such things had all been stated before, and to complain that their retelling strikes no note of new emphasis or re-interpretation?

PLATE 42.—THE MYSTIC MARRIAGE OF ST. CATHERINE : Gerard David.

PLATE 43.—ARTIST UNKNOWN (15TH CENTURY)
FLEMISH (?) OR EARLY FRENCH SCHOOL

"THE LEGEND OF ST. GILES"

THIS picture obviously harks back to the tradition of the monkish illuminators. It is full of the detail upon which they delighted to expend their skill. St. Giles, the founder of a monastery in France, and the patron of cripples and beggars, and all who like them made claims upon his protection, is seen to the right in the dress of a hermit, defending a hind from a royal hunting party. The arrow intended for the quarry has pierced the saint's right hand.

Those who came to hunt have remained to pray, and while it is easy to account for the presence of the richly clad huntsmen and their retainers, the very devout cleric in a white surplice is harder to relate to the scene. This is one of those mediæval panels wherein the artists delighted to mingle the sacred and the secular. It is quaint and odd and beautiful. The tree serves to divide the composition into two halves. To the left are grouped the gentlemen of the chase, to the right the saint with the animal which has sought sanctuary in his arms. Behind him is a strange rocky outcrop and a distance of soft greyish blues. The buildings of a town on a hill can be seen in the left background.

This picture is specially memorable for its cool greens of plant life. How exquisite are the irises, and all the sorrels and parsleys, and the green shooting plant on the right. The reds and blacks of the dresses set off this lucent vegetation. Many of the faces are miniature portraits full of characterization.

Pictures like this belong very obviously to another age than ours. They are archaic, with the romantic qualities we associate with that word. They are naïve in their acceptance of the miraculous, or to say the least, the improbable. Any child would like this work, though it might be difficult for us to answer all the questions it might suggest to a seven-year-old mind.

We can admire it for its highly pictorial qualities, for its sensitive detail, and for that curious blending of the actual and the supernatural, so alien to our modern outlook, and without which so much of our tolerant agnosticism seems lacking in something which only credulity can give.

PLATE 43.—THE LEGEND OF ST. GILES: Flemish School.

PLATE 44.—HANS HOLBEIN THE YOUNGER (1497-1543)
GERMAN SCHOOL

" THE AMBASSADORS "

THE German School, it must be admitted, is not on the whole well represented in the National Gallery. It is a pity, for although the more modern growth of German art has not fulfilled the promise of its early days, those beginnings, from the School of Cologne where the Van Eycks learnt so much, leading on through the engravings of Martin Schoengauer to the genius of Dürer, the one German who has put his country decisively on the artistic map, and who by the magic of his line challenges comparison with the greatest, have an undoubted importance and interest. Unfortunately we have no illustrations either of Dürer in his apocalyptic might, or of Cranach, that playful and exquisite creator whose slender female nudes, with their impudent ivory limbs and small incisive heads, can never be forgotten. When we touch the German School in the person of Hans Holbein the Younger, we touch upon it at the moment when it has come to a plenitude that already bears the seeds of its decline.

His father was Hans Holbein, a painter of the Augsburg School, whose fame is eclipsed by the genius of his much greater son. Hans the Younger was born at Augsburg in 1497, and died in London in 1543. He came first to England in 1526 with letters of introduction to Sir Thomas More. He spent two years in this country, then went back to Basle, but in 1532 returned as court painter to Henry VIII., which post he held until his death.

At one time this country was rich in his portraits, but the majority of them have passed to other lands, and of the few which remain the National Gallery possesses but two. One of these is " The Ambassadors " of our illustration. From its size we might expect a masterpiece, but it must be confessed that this work is a disappointing one. The two figures, painted with that skill and perspicacity which we associate with Holbein, are not really united into a single pictorial whole. He has endeavoured to do this by the table, strewn with a diversity of musical instruments, and by the perspectively distorted image of a human skull, reminiscent of death, lying upon the tessellated floor. He does not succeed, however, and in spite of its almost Venetian richness of colouring this picture leaves us cold. He was, indeed, an unequal painter, but at its best his work has a felicity which entitles him to the place he holds among the greatest portraiturists of all time.

PLATE 44.—THE AMBASSADORS: Holbein the Younger.

PLATE 45.—ARTIST UNCERTAIN (15TH CENTURY)
GERMAN SCHOOL

"PORTRAIT OF A LADY"

THE ascription of this portrait is uncertain. It is undoubtedly German, and has been assigned to Michael Wohlgemut, the tutor and master of Dürer. As such it belongs to the Southern German School, centred round Nuremberg, but the sources of German art are so various and involved that we cannot enter upon them in the space at our disposal. It will be better to confine our attention to this interesting work, and to note a few of its intrinsic qualities. For the sake of chronology, however, we may fix its date about the decade 1485–95.

The first impression may be one of an excessive hardness. There is no softening of line, no gradation between light and dark. This is especially noticeable in the delineation of the hands, which stand out almost detachedly from their background. (They happen to be very shapely, if a little clumsily drawn.) The head-dress with its wide, white linen wings is a prominent feature. It is treated in a dry starched manner, without any of the elaborate folds that so often lend a grace to such apparel. Yet it is entirely in keeping with the spirit of this work. The artist has concentrated upon the vivid face of his sitter, and, as if to emphasize his purpose, has almost encircled it by the stiff white pleats whose lines enclose the features of which they are the foil.

She is very obviously alive. We are aware of her personality, which has been conveyed to us by a singular economy of means. The scant details are precise and exact, the golden pendant hanging from her neck, and the etiolated flower (is it forget-me-not?) which she holds in her left hand. The spacing of the whole design within its frame is remarkably happy.

These qualities arrest us and make us wish to know more. When this has been done we know that we have a vital, though, in this case, it may not be a specially important work of art.

45

PLATE 45.—PORTRAIT OF A LADY: German School.

PLATE 46.—SIR PETER PAUL RUBENS (1577–1640)
LATE FLEMISH SCHOOL

" LANDSCAPE : AUTUMN—THE CHÂTEAU DE STEEN "

THE early Flemish School, as we have noted, was conspicuous for its finish, but the very precision of that strict and meticulous manner ended by becoming a restraint. Breughel was one of the first to let in a breath of wider air. His vigorous peasant types brought new blood to a rather inbred stock, and his amazing passages of landscape, wherein realism and a strange poetic romance were so subtly intermixed, suggested fresh horizons. But it was the genius of Rubens that broke once and for all the fetters of the earlier style. He had travelled extensively, and was one of the few Northern artists who have profited by a study of Italian art. The powerful draughtsmanship of Michelangelo, the rich colour and fluent handling of the Venetians, left their imprint upon his highly receptive mind. An artist of lesser power might under such influences have become a mere eclectic. But Rubens was a Titan. He learnt without imitating, and what he assimilated he transformed.

The friend and counsellor of princes, he was at once ambassador and artist, while his lofty patronage gave him the opportunity of painting those large and sumptuous works, rivalling in scale and virtuosity of execution the most magnificent canvases of Veronese and Tintoretto.

His name is not usually associated with landscape-painting, and for that reason this picture is of special interest. He has painted here his own country residence, the Château de Steen near Mechlin, seen among the trees to the left. In the foreground a wagon is fording a brook, and a sportsman with his gun and dog is stealthily approaching a covey of partridges. Beyond stretches a wide plain merging into an ethereal distance. The whole scene is bathed in a warm autumnal glow, and the afternoon sky, with its suggestion of breezy freshness, is something that had never before been expressed in art. The composition of the picture is singularly spontaneous and arresting. Is it fantasy to suggest that one is aware of something remembered, something vaguely familiar, recovered in an almost Proustian sense, and investing the actual scene with a significance that is more than its intrinsic right ?

To us this picture should be of particular interest. It is the forerunner of the art of Crome and Constable, and when we admire their work we should not be unmindful of a long outstanding debt.

46

PLATE 46.—LANDSCAPE: AUTUMN—THE CHÂTEAU DE STEEN: Rubens.

PLATE 47.—SIR PETER PAUL RUBENS (1577-1640)
LATE FLEMISH SCHOOL

"LE CHAPEAU DE PAILLE"

RUBENS is most typically himself in those large canvases full of movement and pageantry, instinct with the pride of life and delight of the eye. His true master was Veronese. Like him he had a superb sense of decorative composition, and could handle lavish masses of colour, now silvery, now sultry in its glow. His greatest works are scored, as it were, for full orchestra. He is a master of the art of climax, of long crescendos, and as such his allegorical and historical paintings gave him the fullest scope for his exuberant genius.

When he turns to portraiture it is as a relaxation. Yet how certain is his touch, how vivid his realization of the flesh. This portrait of Susanne Fourment, usually known as the " Chapeau de Paille," is an admirable illustration of his powers. She was a sister of Rubens's second wife, and a niece of his first.

He has painted her in a black dress with red sleeves and a dull green scarf thrown over her shoulders. She wears a black Spanish beaver hat trimmed with feathers. The title is a misnomer, a corruption of " Chapeau d'Espagne." It would be more correctly called the " Chapeau de Poil."

Under its wide brim her lustrous eyes look out. The cool and delicate flesh tints are achieved so subtly as to convey an illusion of real flesh and blood. We could easily imagine the colour coming and going in her face, so fully alive does she seem.

Not the least remarkable thing about this portrait is Rubens's treatment of the lighting. She is bathed in reflected sunshine, and the effect is one of open air as opposed to studio lighting. How audacious this work must have seemed when contrasted with the hard mechanical conventions of his Flemish contemporaries.

47

PLATE 47.—LE CHAPEAU DE PAILLE: Rubens.

Plate 48.—SIR PETER PAUL RUBENS (1577–1640)
LATE FLEMISH SCHOOL

"THE JUDGMENT OF PARIS"

IN May 1629 Rubens landed at Greenwich on a diplomatic mission to Charles I. The year before he had been at the Court of Philip IV. of Spain, where he had met Velazquez. His English visit brought him many honours. He was commissioned to decorate the ceiling of Inigo Jones's Banqueting House at Whitehall. The University of Cambridge conferred on him the degree of Master of Arts, and Charles raised him to a knighthood. All his life he was a man of affairs as well as an artist. He worked rapidly, but inevitably had to employ a regiment of pupils and skilled workmen to enable him to carry out his numerous undertakings. Fortunately the Rubens at the National Gallery are undoubtedly from the master's own hand.

Our "Rape of the Sabines" shows him at the plenitude of his powers. Its swirling turbulent composition, carried out with a virtuosity of brushwork and a command of luminous and strangely delicate colour, makes a masterpiece. "The Judgment of Paris" suffers a little by comparison with the other work, but it is an admirable example of his mature style.

Minerva, Venus, and Juno are engaged in displaying their somewhat opulent charms to the rustic Paris, who with his dog and shepherd's crook is reclining at the foot of a tree, with Mercury in attendance. He has already made his momentous decision, and is about to present the apple to Venus, whose flattered expectancy contrasts with the incipient chagrin of her rivals. Minerva is seen with her shield, and Juno with her peacock. In the sky hovers Discord, the authoress of the dissension. The colouring is rich and fluent. The vinous reds to which Rubens inclined in his later period are apparent. There are glimpses of a pleasing pastoral setting. The ladies are rather florid. It cannot be denied that Rubens shows a distinct preference for a more than ample allure. They are scarcely Grecian in their buxomness. It is curious to reflect that this type of nudity has long been accepted as an orthodoxy by the type of mind that was shocked beyond words at the spare svelte body of Manet's "Olympia." An established reputation can be made to cover a multitude of sins.

PLATE 48.—THE JUDGMENT OF PARIS : Rubens.

PLATE 49.—SIR ANTHONY VAN DYCK (1599–1641)
LATE FLEMISH SCHOOL

"PORTRAIT OF A NOBLEMAN"

IN 1615 there entered the studio of Rubens a youth of sixteen who was destined to become his most famous pupil. Anthony Van Dyck was born at Antwerp in 1599. His talents declared themselves at an early age, and he made good use of the opportunities that were his under such a master.

In 1621 he set out for Italy, where he spent seven years. This portrait of Il Marchese Giovanni Battista Cattaneo was painted during his Genoese period.

Van Dyck is first and foremost a portrait-painter. He was never much attracted either to subject pictures or to landscape. The practice of portraiture, especially the portraiture of the world of fashion, is one that has always had its attendant pitfalls. The temptation to flatter, to conform to contemporary taste, is ever present, and from this it cannot be said that Van Dyck entirely escaped. Inevitably he was bound to make certain concessions to his aristocratic patrons. He does it very subtly, however. He had a natural distinction of style; his subjects were for the most part persons of breeding, and when he painted them it was only to be expected that he should endow them with a sense of dignity and reticence that is one of the features of his work. But he is much too great ever to become a mere society painter. He had a power of intellectual penetration and analysis which never forsakes him. This portrait shows how masterly it was.

His earlier pictures have a somewhat limited colour range. All, indeed, are full of his sense of the value of light and shade, but when we come to his lovely "George and Francis Villiers" (3605) the splendour of glowing reds, of tissue of gold, of silvery silken blue is added to a design which in itself is one of his noblest creations. These ill-starred and exceedingly beautiful youths, with their flowing locks and subtle tapering hands, are painted with a lofty pride, touched with a strange tenderness, a note of presage as it were, that makes one feel Van Dyck was inspired with a prophetic insight. This work was painted during his residence in England. He came to this country in 1632 as court painter to Charles I., and died in London in 1641.

PLATE 49.—PORTRAIT OF A NOBLEMAN: Van Dyck.

PLATE 50.—FRANS HALS (1580 ?–1666)
DUTCH SCHOOL

"A FAMILY GROUP"

WITH Frans Hals we come to the first of the Dutch painters illustrated in this book. There are few Dutch pictures extant contemporaneous with the work of the Van Eycks and their immediate successors. The Reformation destroyed in Holland, as in England, the majority of the religious paintings of that period. So when Dutch painters come to our notice, early in the seventeenth century, we find them already possessed of a technical accomplishment, and fully fledged as it were. They had attained a high skill in portraiture and genre-painting, which, with landscape, were the fields in which they were to win their most conspicuous laurels.

Jansz van Mierevelt is the earliest Dutch portrait-painter represented in the gallery. It must be confessed that he is rather dull, conscientious to be sure (the Dutch nearly always are), but that excellent moral quality does not redeem his work from the commonplace.

Frans Hals was a different personality. To English people he will always be associated with his brilliant "Laughing Cavalier" in the Wallace Collection. It is an amazing *tour de force*—a little superficial, perhaps, but possessed of an immense vitality. That smiling, slightly sneering face, with its insolence, its gusto, its air of devil-may-care, is not easily forgotten. Neither is his dashing apparel. Hals is at his best when he confines his attention to a single subject. He never fully mastered the art of composition, and this "Family Group," for all the acumen of his observation, remains a failure. Any one can see how unhappy is its arrangement. The figures are crowded together, leaving an entirely incongruous and meaningless lacuna to the left of the picture. One can expatiate on their individual characterization—one critic has commented on the significance of their varying hands—but the merely accurate announcement of a family tree does not constitute a work of art. It is true that in this conglomerate we possess a more ambitiously extensive Frans Hals than any work of his outside of the great "Archer" groups at Haarlem. But the discerning will turn to the smaller portraits which reveal his consummate handling. And the majority will prefer to remember him as the creator of the "Laughing Cavalier."

PLATE 50.—A FAMILY GROUP : Frans Hals.

PLATE 51.—REMBRANDT (1606–1669)

DUTCH SCHOOL

"PORTRAIT OF AN OLD LADY IN BLACK"

REMBRANDT'S genius is something unique. He remains detached from his Dutch contemporaries. Few painters have penetrated the mystery of life so deeply. No other works are haunted, as are some of his, by a like suffering. In a figurative as well as a literal sense he had looked upon darkness, and looked so long and searchingly that he discovered light.

He was born in 1606 at Leyden, where his father was a miller. One of his earliest masters was Pieter Lastman, an Italianizer with little claim to distinction. The work of Gerard Honthorst, much influenced by the heavy realism of Caravaggio, claimed his attention, but from the outset Rembrandt had a vision of his own. He was specially drawn to a certain aspect of light. Not the brilliant scintillating radiance of Vermeer, nor yet those qualities of lighting that were to interest the Impressionists, but light seen in a conflict with darkness—the illumination of a ray penetrating through gloom, and touching the figures or the objects upon which it falls with a mysterious and dramatic emphasis. That, more than anything else, became the distinctive note of his imagination, and his handling was directed towards its realization in paint. One could almost say that he painted light by an accumulation of darkness.

He had early discovered that a simplification of his palette assisted him in accomplishing the effects he sought. Many of his works are executed almost in a monochrome. He used rich browns and blacks with a masterly sense of their sombre harmonies. Our " Philosopher," a small work and the earliest Rembrandt we possess, is very typical both of his vision and his methods.

This portrait was painted when he was twenty-eight. Youth has rarely shown such an understanding of crabbed age. His sensitive brushwork has delineated every wrinkle, every puckering of the flesh, and caught the resolute fire of those aged and watery eyes. The effect is one of a veteran vigour. The note of suffering is present. Rembrandt's observation is never superficial. He goes to the core of life, and for that reason his portraits move us as few others can.

PLATE 51.—PORTRAIT OF AN OLD LADY IN BLACK: Rembrandt.

PLATE 52.—REMBRANDT (1606–1669)

DUTCH SCHOOL

"SELF-PORTRAIT AT AN ADVANCED AGE"

IN 1634 Rembrandt married Saskia van Uylenborch, the daughter of a successful advocate. It was a happy marriage. She brought him not only good looks and the high spirits of youth, but a share of this world's goods, which enabled him to follow the bent of his own genius untrammelled by the demands of exacting patrons. How far this was to lead him can be realized from his religious paintings, such as the " Christ before Pilate," or " The Adoration of the Shepherds," both in the National Gallery. Sir Charles Holmes makes the rather sweeping statement " that not one of the great Italians has rendered the spirit of Christianity with the same irresistible truth. Fra Angelico has glorified for us the beauty of holiness, Michelangelo has embodied in immortal forms the Creation of Man and the mystery of Death." He is careful to note their several excellences, " but Rembrandt's vision is the widest and deepest of all." It is a matter of personal opinion. I would suggest that Christianity received its most profound expression in Byzantinism, and the work of Giotto and Fra Angelico. Sir Charles adds in quotation, " To Rembrandt the supernatural is inconceivable except in relation to the natural. If man cannot exist without God, God cannot be made manifest except through man." But humanity we have with us always. It is present in Manet's work as well as in Rembrandt's. The Byzantines and the primitive Italians realized something that is superterrestrial, the Word made flesh indeed, but a flesh which seems to be transfigured by that incarnation. That Rembrandt's humanity is so poignant as to move us with its spiritual significance I do not deny. But I find this in his tender painting of his young son Titus, at Hertford House, just as much, and even more than I do in his religious pictures. His genius is religious, in the sense that Dostoievsky's was, but to the sudden illumination that came to St. Paul on the road to Damascus, or to St. Augustine under the fig tree in the garden through the prayers of Monica, he has nothing that is comparable. Fra Angelico, and Giotto, and, in a much later age, El Greco have. The modern humanist is always in danger of forgetting the miracle of revelation.

We have wandered from the subject of this almost excessively human portrait, but the reader will pardon the slight inconvenience if we deal with it along with our next illustration. We have not been digressing from Rembrandt's self.

PLATE 52.—SELF-PORTRAIT: Rembrandt.

PLATE 53.—REMBRANDT (1606-1669)
DUTCH SCHOOL

"PORTRAIT OF AN OLD LADY"

AFTER a few short years of happy married life, bereavement and poverty became the lot of Rembrandt. The sorrow caused by the death of two infant daughters and a son was deepened by the loss of his mother. Saskia herself died after several illnesses in 1642.

Rembrandt's highly personal style, his predilection for shadow in place of vivid colouring, were not qualities likely to establish him as a popular portrait-painter. What was his loss has been the world's gain. One wonders if the large number of portraits he painted of himself may in part be accounted for by a dearth of sitters. Our last portrait of himself, at an advanced age, shows him as one who has weathered the storms and hardships of life. It is full of suffering. A similar poignancy is in the portrait of Titus to which we have referred. His love for the boy expresses itself in a miraculous tenderness that has passed into every rapid stroke of his brush. "The child is father of the man," and the short-lived Titus is present here in his father's ageing face. Certainly this portrait is full of brooding memories. The plain and rather shabby clothes tell of his poverty in everything else but the things of the spirit. And is there not a certain loneliness in this picture, a solitude of soul that belongs to those who have fathomed life so fully?

This "Old Lady" on the opposite page reveals a like insight into age. Of Rembrandt's technical qualities as such, we have not room to speak. His handling of light alone would provide material for a chapter. In his later work he loads his brush with colour, and applies it with a vehemence always directed by his undeviating sense of purpose. Such a style, however, could not expect to find favour with patrons accustomed to the meticulous surface finish of De Hooch and the other painters of cabinet pictures.

No mention of Rembrandt is complete without some reference to his drawings and etchings. He is probably the greatest etcher who ever lived, and a visit to the British Museum is a necessary supplement to any study of his paintings at Trafalgar Square.

PLATE 53.—PORTRAIT OF AN OLD LADY: Rembrandt.

PLATE 54.—GERARD TERBORCH (1617–1681)
DUTCH SCHOOL

"THE PEACE OF MÜNSTER"

TERBORCH is chiefly remembered for his conversation pieces, those exquisitely painted interiors wherein are shown well-to-do Dutch people occupying themselves with music or other social pursuits. We have admirable examples of this pleasing art in our illustrations of De Hooch and Metsu and Vermeer, and for that reason these two rather unique paintings of Terborch are interesting as showing his talent in another field.

"The Peace of Münster" is first and foremost an historical document. It is exceedingly well painted and planned, but the pleasure we derive from it is not an æsthetic one. In this work the artist takes second place to the archivist. He is bent upon setting down minutely, and with the greatest possible realism, a record of a highly important national event. The long and bitter religious wars are over, and Philip IV. of Spain has been obliged to recognize the independence of the Dutch United Provinces. The draft treaty had been drawn up at Osnabrück on the 30th of January previously. This represents the solemn ratifying and confirming by oath of the articles of peace by the plenipotentiaries of Spain and the delegates of the United Provinces, who assembled for this purpose in the Rathaus at Münster on May 15, 1648. The Spaniards are seen resting their hands on a copy of the Gospels open on the table before them. The six Dutch representatives are holding up their right hands in assent. They all seem highly conscious of the solemnity of the occasion. Each one of the heads is a miniature portrait, obviously studied from life, for a close inspection reveals a high degree of individual characterization.

A pictorial unity is given to the scene by the mellow lighting, a golden tone which is added to by the wainscotted wall in the background, and by the elaborate chandelier which bears a representation in metal of the Madonna and Child.

A modern counterpart of this picture can be seen in Sir William Orpen's brilliant "Signing of the Peace Treaties at Versailles." It is interesting to note how the modern technician approaches a similar subject. If Orpen's delineation of detail is less minute, his handling is much freer. He has used the glittering magnificence of the Hall of the Mirrors to provide a setting in which the assembled statesmen are dwarfed by its splendour, and the contrast results in a note of subtle cynicism, singularly absent in the almost religious gravity of this earlier work.

PLATE 54.—THE PEACE OF MÜNSTER: Gerard Terborch.

PLATE 55.—GERARD TERBORCH (1617–1681)
DUTCH SCHOOL

" PORTRAIT OF A GENTLEMAN "

ONE cannot help liking this grave young gentleman, whose black cloak seems to be opening like a parachute, and whose calves are hidden in flounces, once thought becoming to that portion of the female anatomy. He is balanced like a teetotum or spinning top upon an invisible axis, springing from the soles of his elaborate *pantouffles*, the shaft, as it were, of all his umbrella-shaped accoutrements. One feels that he could equally well shut up or open out wider, with what Alice-in-Wonderland effects one would not care to say. Take away the table and the chair, which lend an apparent support to the composition, and he could hardly stand upright except for some gyroscopic momentum, or since this is obviously absent, unless he were a tailor's dummy.

This is a small portrait, measuring only some two feet square. If it were enlarged to life-size the result would be definitely disquieting.

To a contemporary of Terborch's, accustomed to see such attire walking about the streets—is he going to church or to a funeral ?—the effect would be less striking. But one is tempted to accredit Terborch with a certain dry sense of humour in this portrait, all the more to his relish, and to ours, because it is so conspicuously lacking in the demure face of the young gentleman.

Those who find a different meaning are probably in the right, and will be able to supply their own gloss. But they could not like this picture better than the writer does, or be more grateful to the young man for the care he has taken with his voluminous attire.

PLATE 55.—PORTRAIT OF A GENTLEMAN: Gerard Terborch.

PLATE 56.—PHILIPS DE KONINCK (1619–1688)
DUTCH SCHOOL

"LANDSCAPE: A VIEW IN HOLLAND"

THE origins of Dutch landscape-painting can be traced back to early Flemish art. The religious painters, as we have seen, delighted to introduce miniature landscapes into the background of their pictures. Breughel carried this a stage further. His landscapes, especially those in which the transit of the seasons is recorded, have a quality all their own, a legendary beauty like that of a folk-song in music.

When the violence of the struggle with Spain abated in the seventeenth century, it was only natural that the Dutch, who loved their country—a country which they had wrested both from the foreigner and the invading sea—should turn their eyes upon it, and begin to paint the scenes around them. The peculiar nature of that landscape lent itself pre-eminently to the painter's art. The level plains, the slow-flowing rivers and canals, the towns and homesteads, all seen under wide and changing skies, were a stretched canvas, as it were, upon which nature worked in her broadest and most luminous effects, a canvas, too, that was crowded with a rich and lively human interest. So in the early Dutch landscapes there is little conscious composition, little attempt at a studied grouping, either of details or masses. The painter set down what was immediately before his eyes, and as a result we often get the panoramic effect noticeable in this picture.

Philips de Koninck is not the earliest of the specifically Dutch painters of landscape. Van Goyen and Van der Neer preceded him, as did Brouwer. Specimens of their work can be studied in the gallery. One would specially like to mention Brouwer's "Tobias and the Angel."

Koninck cannot be considered a subtle painter, but he is honest and straightforward. This "View in Holland" catches the salient features of a typically Dutch scene. He is not quite certain as to how he really wishes to treat his foreground. His eye was on the distance, and it is those cold blue spears of land and water and reflected light, spread along the horizon, that are the most beautiful things in this picture. The rather sullen light cast down from the sky gives a unity of mood to the extensive and rather diffuse panorama, and we get a sense of air and space, if no highly imaginative or arresting moments, from this landscape.

PLATE 56.—VIEW IN HOLLAND : Philips de Koninck.

PLATE 57.—AELBERT CUYP (1620–1691)
DUTCH SCHOOL

"CATTLE AND FIGURES"

CUYP was one of the earliest landscape-painters to become enamoured of sunlight. He sought to distil it from the air and suffuse his canvases with its tincture. For this reason he has been called the Dutch Claude, but there the similarity ends. Cuyp is much more homely in his choice of subjects. He painted the fields and pastures round Dordrecht just as he saw them. When we think of him we immediately think of cows; they occur again and again in his compositions. No other painter has given that bovine animal such an exalted place in art.

Four of them are seen in this very typical Cuyp of our illustration. It is milking-time, and a milkmaid is pouring the fresh milk into large earthenware pots. Two men appear on the hillock above her, and in the background are a windmill and the church and town of Dordrecht.

There is a lovely lemon-yellow glow of light in the sky and the aerial distance. The same glint touches the flanks of the cow lying in the foreground, and sparkles like dew on the briers. At first sight one might think that Cuyp had solved the problem of open-air naturalistic lighting. But much of the picture is distinctly dark and heavy in tone. It lacks the vitality we expect from real sunlight. But the truth is, his sunlight is like an alchemist's extract, a varnish, as it were, that he applies in a rather formulated manner to give a golden effect indeed, but one that falls far short of the magic of nature. There is something rather drowsy about Cuyp's charm. He is somewhat ruminative like his lethargic animals, a little too bucolic—with the heaviness the ancients were wont to associate with that word. Yet he is honest, a scrupulous workman with a flair for composition, and he did want to paint sunlight.

He succeeded only partially, as is often the lot of pioneers, but his canvases have been a source of inspiration to later painters, among them our own John Crome, and others of the Norwich School. And over and above all this his pictures are pleasing in themselves.

PLATE 57.—CATTLE AND FIGURES: Cuyp.

PLATE 58.—GABRIEL METSU (1630 ?–1667)
DUTCH SCHOOL

"THE MUSIC LESSON"

WITH this exquisite picture of Metsu's we come to the first of our Dutch conversation pieces. Sir Charles Holmes has suggested that the idea of an open window gives the clue to the secret of the Netherland cabinet paintings. He stresses the reactions of the long northern winter which compelled one to remain indoors, and when indoors meant the relatively small rooms of Dutch town houses, pictures that gave an extension to one's horizon, that let in glimpses of other scenes, would naturally be valued. The term looking-glass might often be better employed, for many, and indeed some of the brightest of these "windows" let into other rooms, are indeed reflections of the room in which they were intended to hang. This might well be so of the "Music Lesson."

It is an exceedingly small painting, measuring only about one foot square. But within that compass how much of poetry is comprised. As with all such works the lighting is an important feature. Here we have not the brilliance of Vermeer but a cool and beautifully luminous quality. Never before were such limpid greys as on the faintly shadowed wall. The mood of the lighting finds its keynote in the lovely Ruisdael landscape hanging in the background, but against this delicate softness Metsu has set vivid touches of pure colour—the lady's scarlet bodice, the man's blue hose, and the rich tablecloth with its tasselled fringe.

The design is a subtle intermixture of rectilinear forms—the long horizontals of the virginal, the sharp pattern of the black-and-white flooring, and the square-set pictures hanging on the wall, blended with the curves of the figures, the lady's buff-coloured skirt, and the man's bent attitude as he inclines to his agreeable pupil.

For all its diminutive size this canvas is not overcrowded. Metsu has chosen just the right amount of incident, and by what a miracle of subtle juxtaposition of tones does he convey the sense of spatial relationship. Other cabinet pictures of this type may be more brilliant in effect (Vermeer's, for example), others more enveloped in the softness that is seen in Metsu's own "Duet," but here he has struck a happy medium. It is one of the most lovely Dutch paintings we possess.

PLATE 58.—THE MUSIC LESSON: Metsu.

PLATE 59.—PIETER DE HOOCH (1629–1677 ?)
DUTCH SCHOOL

"INTERIOR OF A DUTCH HOUSE"

BY a curious paradox, the most brilliant handling of light in
Dutch art has been achieved in paintings of interiors. The
limitations of the space upon which it plays, the brightness
of the dresses, and the various objects which arrest its glitter,
all contribute to this result. And it must be remembered
that outdoor art was as yet only feeling its way, and that painters (even
Vermeer in his lovely luminous " View of Delft ") had not yet attempted
to paint sunshine in its full intoxicating glare. Claude's suns seem to
be either rising or setting, and they are mellow with that transience.
But De Hooch, here in a wine-glass held in a woman's hand, has focused
light, caught it in its diamond brilliance, and it may well be that the
uplifted arm of the gaudily dressed cavalier is saluting that marvel.

This work is a milestone on the road to the art of Vermeer. The
picture needs so little description that one may pause to consider how
it differs from painting as it was conceived of by the Italians. One
must be chary of generalizations, but on the whole Italian painting
inclined to the sculpturesque. Volume and movement, and all the
subtleties that bind these two together, were the dominating principles
upon which they built their art. (Incidentally they are the greatest,
the most moving, qualities capable of translation into pictorial form.)

The Dutch had before them a different ideal, closer to reality, that
is reality as immediately seen. They did not seek for any transposition,
and they are happiest when they have succeeded in investing reality
with a stimulating appeal, arising from the intrinsic qualities of the
subject depicted, rather than from any passionate vision imposed upon
it, bringing by its very domination an arbitrary glory more akin to the
world of ideas than to that of fact.

De Hooch in this picture has fully realized what he set out to
paint. The felicity of his composition needs no emphasis. One trivial
yet significant detail remains to be noted. The thinness of the film of
paint which he used to ensnare light in its meshes is so fragile that
with age it has become transparent, and the tessellated flooring shows
through the maidservant's skirt. That in itself is a comment upon
this highly nervous and meticulous art.

PLATE 59.—INTERIOR OF A DUTCH HOUSE: de Hooch.

PLATE 60.—PIETER DE HOOCH (1629–1677 ?)
DUTCH SCHOOL

"COURT OF A DUTCH HOUSE"

IN this picture we have De Hooch out of doors. He is much less magical than he was within. Not that this work is without its qualities of lighting, but it is the diffused brightness affected by the most conscientious of the pre-Raphaelites, casting few shadows, and for that very reason robbed of its moments of charm. The lady who held the scintillating wine-glass in her hand is here seen in the passage-way—at least, the woman who stands there is dressed in the same attire. But she is less prominent than the other, who leads the little girl towards us. They make a very engaging pair, and indeed there is nothing in this picture that does not immediately claim our attention. If one were numerically minded one could count the paving stones and the pleasant geranium red bricks.

I do not wish to belittle this picture, or to detract from its very happy and entirely natural composition, but the fact remains that if ever colour photography surmounts the technical obstacles that seem to beset its progress, it would be capable of giving us a result not widely different from this. And that consummation would not be art. Since this picture antedates the camera by some two hundred years, De Hooch was doing something that could be done no other way. And there is present a note of intimacy that no purely mechanical process could give.

Here is, if you will, the open window, but this particular window does little more than frame what it views. It is not a magic casement, and those who are moved by this work (in so far as they are not engrossed by its very high technical ability) will be moved by its representational quality, and not by any indwelling mind that might raise it from literalism to the altogether different plane of creation.

PLATE 60.—COURT OF A DUTCH HOUSE: de Hooch.

PLATE 61.—JAN VERMEER VAN DELFT (1632-1675)
DUTCH SCHOOL

"A YOUNG LADY AT A SPINET"

THE three preceding plates form an appropriate introduction to this very striking genre piece by Vermeer van Delft. He was a contemporary of Metsu and De Hooch, and like them drew his subjects very largely from scenes of the comfortable domestic life of his well-to-do fellow citizens.

He left comparatively few works behind him, and we are fortunate to possess in "A Young Lady at a Spinet" a canvas that reveals his mastery, especially in his unique handling of light. It streams in from the window on the left, setting the small framed landscape on the wall aglow, and glittering with a reflected glory on the silks and fine array of the young woman who is the centre of interest in this very dazzling picture. It is not so full of incident as Metsu's "Music Lesson," with which it at once suggests comparison. Metsu's painting is pitched in a lower key, the lighting though admirably handled being more subdued.

Vermeer revelled in luminosity. His canvases radiate light; not the studied and artificial lighting of the studio, but pure and unalloyed sunshine. He was also an adept in his rendering of fabrics and textures. Notice the brilliant painting of the satin dress and the blue silk bodice the young lady is wearing. The colour seems to vibrate. One forgets that it is pigment, so amazing is the skill with which it has been handled.

The composition of the picture is singularly formal. The figure occupies the centre of the canvas, which is almost bisected vertically by the line of the body, continued upwards in the jet-black picture frame. The lady's attention seems to be divided between her playing and the fact that she is being painted. Her pose is somewhat stiff, especially in relation to the spinet, whose sharp rectilinear form seems to emphasize a quite deliberate angularity. In the hands of a lesser painter the effect might have been a little awkward, and even as it is, the placing of the figure of Cupid is not particularly happy.

But the glory of this picture is in its colour — turquoise blue, delicate apple-greens, and the touches of crimson that heighten the brilliancy of the dress. Vermeer's virtuosity is such that it appears quite effortless. In sheer delight of the eye few, if any, have surpassed him.

PLATE 61.—A YOUNG LADY AT A SPINET: Vermeer Van Delft.

PLATE 62.—NICOLAES MAES (1632–1693)
DUTCH SCHOOL

"THE IDLE SERVANT"

NICOLAES MAES was a pupil of Rembrandt. From him he acquired a love of chiaroscuro, though he never learnt to handle that dangerous artifice with the profundity of his master. What was in Rembrandt almost a law of his imagination becomes in Maes merely a mannerism, a trick of emphasis. He concentrates his high lights upon the figure or group of figures which he wishes to bring into prominence, and fills in the background with dark shadows, often warm and pleasantly atmospheric in their effect, but in this picture inclined to turn into a brown fog that soaks up light like a sponge, and blurs rather than stresses the contrasts he intended to produce.

The subject is treated with a good-natured sense of humour. Hogarth would have given us a much more racy version, but we are arrested by the episode, and the two chief figures are rendered in an exceedingly life-like way. Less happy is the glimpse of the farther room. The murk to which we have referred has settled there quite unmistakably. His painting lacks crispness of touch, and the result is a rather woolly texture.

The truth is that the virtue of genre pictures of this type, and of the relatively small-scale Dutch conversation pieces, depends to a great extent on the vivacity of the artist's handling and the perfection of his finish. When these are not of an outstanding quality there is often little left, beyond some passing pleasure of anecdote, to claim our attention.

PLATE 62.—THE IDLE SERVANT: Maes.

PLATE 63.—MEINDERT HOBBEMA (1638–1709)
DUTCH SCHOOL

"THE AVENUE, MIDDELHARNIS"

NO reference to Dutch landscape-painting can afford to omit the name of Ruisdael. He is not represented in this volume, but the reader can turn to the picture hanging on the wall of Metsu's "Music Lesson" (Plate 58) to see something of the sombre harmonies of light he made so peculiarly his own. He never painted direct sunlight; nearly all his pictures are a little overcast with ebony shadows and heavy passages of woodland, but they are full of cool silvery lights, and are informed by a delicate poetic sense, a note of loneliness, to which they owe much of their charm.

Hobbema was influenced by him, not very happily at first. He inclined to crowd his pictures with leafage, treated in a rather fussy conventional way. One remembers Ruskin's exaggerated comment, " A single dusty roll of Turner's brush is more truly expressive of the infinity of foliage than all the niggling of Hobbema."

Curiously enough it was after Hobbema had abandoned his career as a struggling artist, and taken a post in the Dutch customs, that he produced his masterpiece, our " Avenue at Middelharnis." It is one of the most popular pictures in the gallery. It is not hard to see how this painting appeals by its straightforwardness. There is a directness in its rectilinear composition that in a lesser artist's hands might well have resulted in stiffness. The long perspective of the avenue flanked by tall slender trees bisects the canvas. A church to the left and some farm buildings to the right supply the only architectural features. The careful husbandry of the Dutch is minutely noted.

This picture delights us by its sense of space. We feel the wide level expanse of the plain, and of the sky with its gently moving clouds. Hobbema's balancing of his bold vertical and less sharply accented horizontal lines renders this three-dimensional quality in a very high degree.

He was one of the painters who influenced our own Norwich School, and for this reason, quite apart from its natural charm, it is appropriate that his masterpiece should hang at Trafalgar Square.

PLATE 63.—THE AVENUE, MIDDELHARNIS : Hobbema.

PLATE 64.—VELAZQUEZ (1599–1660)

SPANISH SCHOOL

"PHILIP IV., KING OF SPAIN"

DON DIEGO DE SILVA VELAZQUEZ (to give him his full name) was born at Seville in 1599. He came of gentle parentage. As a boy he entered the studio of Herrera the Elder, who is remembered chiefly for his ill-temper. A kindlier master was found in the gentle if rather insignificant Pacheo, and under his supervision the young man who was destined to become a prince among court painters curiously enough began his career by painting a series of *bodegones*, or kitchen scenes, then very much the vogue. Our " Christ in the House of Martha " belongs to this period. In 1623 he was introduced to the court, and Philip IV. gave him the first of many sittings. Rubens visited Madrid in 1628, and advised the brilliant young artist to travel in Italy. Velazquez's style had sufficiently formed by then for him to do this without allowing his own personality to be merged in a composite of the great Venetians and later Florentines. He possibly learnt something from Veronese's silvery colouring and subtle use of impasto. His Italian visit did not, however, shackle him with the studious acquisitions of an eclectic ; it quickened his own innate perception, and added a note of animation to his already solid and masterly execution. This can be seen from his " Philip IV. when Young," painted immediately on his return from Italy. The silver brocade of his court dress is painted with an amazing vivacity. In spite of the conventions of ceremonial portraiture Velazquez has succeeded in creating a work full of vitality as well as dignity.

Some twenty-five years separate the Philip IV. of our illustration from the earlier portrait. In the meanwhile the king has aged not a little, and the painter's art deepened in its insight.

The note of this picture is one extreme quiet. The king is dressed simply in a rich black robe sparingly embroidered with gold. He wears a plain stiff collar and the narrow chain and badge of the Order of the Golden Fleece. The face is painted in soft flesh tones with touches of delicate silvery impasto. The heavy Hapsburg chin is forgotten when we look at the majestic lion-like forehead. He is tired and disillusioned, but he is every inch a king. Few portraits have ever so marvellously represented gentleness and at the same time an inscrutable pride, all the more secure because of its reticence and lofty calm.

PLATE 64.—PHILIP IV. OF SPAIN: Velasquez.

PLATE 65.—VELAZQUEZ (1599–1660)

SPANISH SCHOOL

"VENUS AND CUPID"

THIS picture, "Venus and Cupid," better known as the Rokeby Venus, from the house in which it formerly had its home, was painted in Velazquez's later period. Paintings of the nude were frowned upon by the Spanish ecclesiastical authorities, and only an artist very firmly established in the royal favour could have dared to produce such a work at that time. An attack was made upon it in the gallery by a fanatic in 1914.

The design is suave and flowing. The long sweep of the draperies below emphasizes the curve of the recumbent figure. The bend of her right arm has a counterpart in the bend of Cupid's knee. His presence to the left of the picture preserves the balance of interest.

The quality of the flesh painting has long been famous. Things like the drawing of the legs, and of the hollow between the shoulder-blades, are evidences of a master.

Velazquez has not attempted to invest the subject with the heroics of the " grand manner." His Venus is not a classical goddess, but a very comely young woman painted from life.

For all its undeniable charm of composition and colouring, one cannot help feeling that there is something shallow about this picture, a certain superficiality of sentiment that we do not associate with Velazquez. It may be a purely personal reaction, and no doubt the majority will find in this pleasantly palpable divinity an abstraction of feminine graces, and the symbol of beauty's self.

PLATE 65.—VENUS AND CUPID : Velasquez.

PLATE 66.—W. HOGARTH (1697–1764)

" THE SHRIMP GIRL "

THE history of painting in England does not present the same continuity of development that we find in countries like Italy or France, or the Netherlands. It received a rude shock at the Reformation, which broke up the school of monkish illuminators and miniature painters, and led to a wholesale destruction of our primitives. Henry VIII., by bringing over Holbein as Court painter, set a fashion that was followed by succeeding monarchs down to the time of William of Orange.

The modern British School may be said to begin with Hogarth, who, as well as being the first, remains for all time one of the greatest of English masters. To many his name primarily suggests the satirist whose pictures of contemporary life and manners exposed the foibles and profligacy of society, both high and low. So much so indeed that one is in danger of overlooking his supreme qualities as a pure artist.

" The Shrimp Girl " reveals him as a painter of extreme sensibility. In technique it is modern. The brushwork is daringly swift and liquid, the colouring aglow with life. He has struck that note of happy naturalism which is one of the outstanding qualities of the English School at its best.

She carries on her head a basket full of shrimps, containing a metal gill measure. Her lips are parted, as though she were crying her wares. Notice the fresh colouring of her cheeks and the roguish twinkle in her eyes. Her dress is treated sketchily, but its tawny russet hues and grey shadows all contribute to the effect as a whole.

No fresher canvas ever came from the hand of any English painter.

" Instead of burdening the memory with musty rules, or tiring the eye with copying dry or damaged pictures, I have ever found studying from nature the shortest and safest way of obtaining knowledge in my art." So he wrote, and " The Shrimp Girl " shows how he carried his creed into practice. Subsequent painters would have done well had they followed his example, instead of pandering to popular taste, especially in the fashionable portraiture of their time.

English art has reached its greatest heights when it has remained true to this simple yet by no means easy maxim. None other has suited our national genius so well.

PLATE 66.—THE SHRIMP GIRL: Hogarth.

PLATE 67.—SIR JOSHUA REYNOLDS (1723–1792)

"THE GRACES DECORATING A TERMINAL FIGURE OF HYMEN"

SIR JOSHUA REYNOLDS was born on July 16, 1723, at Plympton near Plymouth, where his father was headmaster of a small grammar school. He began to draw at an early age, and there still exists a sketch of his done on the back of a Latin exercise and bearing in his father's writing the very parental admonition, "This is drawn by Joshua in school, out of pure idleness." His father was divided in his mind as to whether to make the boy an apothecary or an artist. In the end it was art that won. At the age of seventeen he was sent up to London to enter the studio of Thomas Hudson. They soon parted company, and the next important event in Joshua's life was his meeting with Captain (afterwards Admiral) Keppel, who took him on a voyage to the Mediterranean. Reynolds spent three years in Italy. He worked assiduously, copying Old Masters and studying their methods, and acquired a love for the " grand manner " which he brought back with him. Success came to him rapidly. He was soon the most popular portrait painter in London.

Portraiture is by its nature one of the most conventional forms of art. Only the greatest masters have been able to rise above its limitations and to make it a vehicle of their own personal expression. Reynolds is not one of these. He had an immense power of application and no small talent. He had a wide knowledge of the conventions, especially those of the " grand manner," and he could handle such clichés with an air of authority. But it is not out of such aptitudes that greatness in art is born.

"The Graces Decorating a Terminal Figure of Hymen " is an admirable example of his fluent rhetoric. They are the three daughters of Sir William Montgomery, the second of whom was engaged to the Hon. Luke Gardiner. Mr. Gardiner wished to have a portrait group of his fiancée and her two sisters, "representing," as he put it, " some emblematical or historical subject." He got what he wanted. As all three young ladies were bespoken in marriage, what happier inspiration than to represent them in the act of decorating the figure of Hymen with the flowery wreath they were shortly themselves to wear. With a becoming elegance and an alacrity that never trespasses upon maidenly reserve, they are seen at their pleasing task.

Notice the way in which the voluminous drapery in the background is intermarried with the trees. A really great baroque painter might have contrived to do something memorable with such an invention. But Sir Joshua is too sober for the abandonment required, and while he succeeds possibly in avoiding the ridiculous, it can scarcely be claimed that he has risen to the sublime.

PLATE 67.—THE GRACES DECORATING A TERMINAL FIGURE: Reynolds.

Plate 68.—SIR JOSHUA REYNOLDS (1723–1792)

"LADY COCKBURN AND HER CHILDREN"

THERE is something of the pedagogue in Reynolds's attitude to painting. It was typical of him that he should have been one of the promoters of the Royal Academy, "for the better cultivation, improvement, and encouragement of painting, sculpture, architecture, and the arts of design in general." It was founded in 1768, with Sir Joshua as its first president. "Cultivation, improvement, and encouragement," the well-meaning words have a somewhat sententious ring, as has the preamble to his famous *Discourses* which were intended "to make and prove art a matter fit to occupy cultivated and serious minds." But indeed the *Discourses*, despite their pedantry, contain quite a deal of shrewd and spirited observation. One is tempted to think of him as the Doctor Johnson of English painting, but he has not the stature of his great contemporary.

A knighthood conferred in 1769 followed upon these highly eminent public services. His diary, under the heading of April 21st of that year, contains the laconic entry: "$12\frac{1}{2}$ King's Levee, knighted at St. James'," and records the fact that he gave sittings to a Miss Norcliffe at 11 o'clock, and to a Mr. Simmonds at 2 on the same day. He was as busy as a fashionable physician, and portrait after portrait came from his hand.

"Lady Cockburn and her Children" was painted in 1773, when he was at the height of his vogue. It is a very pleasant picture. Although he never married, he had a highly sympathetic appreciation of feminine charm and a real feeling for children.

Lady Cockburn, wearing a white dress and a saffron-coloured mantle trimmed with a border of fur, sits surrounded by her three young sons. A parrot is painted in loud colours against the base of a column on the right Conventional draperies form the background, which includes a peep of landscape.

Mr. Manson, in his excellent book *The Tate Gallery*, commenting on the English portrait painters of the eighteenth century, remarks that "they have a reputation out of all proportion to their purely artistic merits. This is partly due to their discovery and exploitation by the dealers. The first big price paid for a Reynolds was in 1821, when his 'Charity' changed hands at £1,155, but for long after that a Reynolds could have been bought at auction for a guinea."

This picture fetched the sum of £24,000 in the year 1900.

PLATE 68.—LADY COCKBURN AND HER CHILDREN: Reynolds.

PLATE 69.—SIR JOSHUA REYNOLDS (1723–1792)

"THE AGE OF INNOCENCE"

THIS popular and charming picture has established itself firmly as a favourite. Nor are the reasons far to seek. It possesses an undeniable appeal. Its pictorial qualities are eked out by a choice of title which supplies just the right touch of sentiment to win its way to the heart of the general public, to whom childhood and innocence are still synonymous terms.

As a matter of fact, Reynolds did have an insight where children are concerned. He painted them with a sympathy and an originality that is only too frequently missing in his conventional portraiture. At times a note of forced sentimentality obtrudes itself, as in the case of his altogether too angelic "Infant Samuel"; but this little maiden, despite her piously clasped hands, remains essentially a really living young human being (we will not say animal), and refuses to exist merely as an allegory of virtue. Her *naïveté* is quite convincing, and there is a welcome absence of sophistication in the harmonious background. Gone are the canopies and columns of the "grand manner," and instead we have a rich, if rather sombre, passage of landscape.

If her pose is somewhat arbitrary and studied, it is at least simple, and builds up a pleasing pyramidal form. Whatever moralization may be implied by the folded hands, he has left her face alone. It is natural and inquisitive, and the whole of the painting of her head with its wayward crop of hair has a distinct freshness.

Unfortunately, this picture is in a bad state of preservation. For all his scientific curiosity he was not over scrupulous in the choice of his own materials, many of which have turned out to be perishable, so that his canvases have faded, cracked, and deteriorated more than those of any of his contemporaries.

As to his ultimate position in English art, that is inevitably a question upon which private judgments will differ. None can overlook his importance and his widespread influence, but to many he will seem deficient in the power of real creation, and few will deny that his reputation to-day is not that which it was in his own age, or as it appeared to many of his followers, who regarded him as no less than an oracle.

PLATE 69.—THE AGE OF INNOCENCE: Reynolds.

PLATE 70.—T. GAINSBOROUGH (1727–1788)

"RALPH SCHOMBERG, ESQ., M.D."

GAINSBOROUGH and Reynolds were contemporaries. They both are remembered chiefly as portrait painters. Inevitably they were influenced by the fashions of their age, used the same idioms, and to a considerable extent shared an identity of aim. But when that is said, the apparent similarity ends. It would be hard to find two artists who have been bracketed together who were in reality more disparate in their approach to art, and in the quality of their most notable achievements. Reynolds remains what is probably our best example of academic eclecticism, Gainsborough as a product of pure personality, singularly unindebted to conscious schooling. He arrived at greatness by his sheer sensitivity, which had for its expression a subtlety of touch unparalleled in the history of English painting.

He was born in Suffolk in the spring of 1727, and his life falls into three chapters, his Ipswich period, his sojourn in Bath, and his closing years in London. Unlike Reynolds, he never travelled abroad. Such influences as there are in his work (and they are at second remove) may be mainly attributed to Rubens and Van Dyck.

As might be expected in the case of such an individualist, his quality is uneven, but when inspired he is one of those rare masters who can lift portraiture to a plane where it becomes the medium of the artist's own creativity. He is happiest when he is painting women, yet this portrait of Ralph Schomberg, M.D., is an admirable example of his art. He is less interested than Reynolds was in masculine characterization. There is no very marked penetration in the painting of the face. The pleasure that this picture gives is not due to any psychological profundity—in fact, this is strangely absent. Gainsborough was as much interested in the court suit of claret-coloured velvet as he was in the doctor's physiognomy. His whole bearing, however, is expressive, and is rendered with a gracious dignity.

The deftness of the execution is apparent everywhere. It is an aristocratic painting, conscious of its poise and good breeding. Beside it much of the most accomplished work of his rivals seems bourgeois and commonplace.

PLATE 70.—RALPH SCHOMBERG, ESQ., M.D.: Gainsborough.

Plate 71.—T. GAINSBOROUGH (1727–1788)

"PORTRAIT OF MRS. SIDDONS"

FOR once, one would like to stray farther afield and be able to include Gainsborough's portrait of the Hon. Mrs. Graham, which is one of the glories of the Edinburgh Gallery. He never surpassed it. Those who have seen either the original or any reasonably adequate reproduction can never forget its amazing loveliness. It affects one like a passage of music. Its delicacy, its elusive and haunting charm derived from a miraculous handling of paint, a quality of texture no other English painter has ever achieved, set it apart, isolated in its perfection, which is quite incommunicable in words.

In our attempt to arrive at an estimation of Gainsborough's genius, one may be pardoned this digression.

The Mrs. Siddons of our illustration is a brilliantly clever work, but it lacks the magical quality of the Edinburgh painting. The celebrated actress is portrayed in her make-up with her hair powdered. She wears a blue-and-white striped dress, and a merry widow hat trimmed with black feathers. The rippling quality of his touch plays with the fabrics, but the note of the picture is epigrammatic rather than lyrical. It suggests comparison with the best French portraiture of the period. Boucher would not come out of the ordeal well, and Fragonard lacks the transparent refinement of the Englishman's work.

Gainsborough, whose happy-go-lucky nature was drawn to Bath by the attractions of that fashionable watering-place, returned to London somewhat hurriedly in 1774 and set up as a portrait painter in Pall Mall. This picture belongs to his London period. His position in the capital was one of rival to Sir Joshua Reynolds, and their relations were not improved by Gainsborough's quarrel with the Royal Academy over the hanging of one of his pictures, and his consequent withdrawal as an exhibitor. They were reconciled, however, at the end.

Gainsborough's contribution to landscape painting is dealt with later. He declared that it was largely force of circumstance that made him devote so much of his time to portraiture. We can hardly regret the necessity, seeing that it has given us so many great works.

PLATE 71.—MRS. SIDDONS: Gainsborough.

PLATE 72.—GEORGE ROMNEY (1734–1802)

"A LADY AND CHILD"

ROMNEY, the third of the trio of eighteenth-century English portrait painters, was in every way inferior to the other two. His reputation, both in his own day, when he succeeded in establishing a fashionable and lucrative connection, and in more recent times, when, thanks largely to the strategy of the dealers, his works have frequently changed hands at sums of four figures, has been out of all proportion to his true artistic worth.

He was a north country man, born at Beckside, near Dalton-in-Furness, and at an early age began to draw. He was apprenticed to a rather mountebank artist named Steele, who moved about from place to place, some say to avoid his creditors, and who in 1755 happened to be practising in Kendal.

Romney married early, his choice falling upon his landlady's daughter, a young woman named Mary Abbott. By her he had two children, one of whom, John, entered Holy Orders and wrote a Memoir of his father. He left his wife behind in Kendal when, in 1762, he set out to seek his fortune in London. In March 1773 we find him doing the correct thing by paying a visit to Italy. His son records of him that "after having examined in Pisa the early works of the venerable Giotto and other old masters," he proceeded to Florence. There are no pictures by Giotto at Pisa, but indeed that is no very grave matter. Romney was hardly likely to be unduly influenced by the art of the *trecento*. In Rome he made a full-sized copy of the lower half of Raphael's "Transfiguration." That sounds a more congenial task, but an unkind critic has reminded us that only the upper part of that picture is accepted as being the work of the great Umbrian master. Clearly the Italian trip might have been more profitably arranged. He returned, however, with the prestige of having visited the birthplace and true nursery of the arts, an asset of considerable cultural and commercial worth to a would-be rival of Reynolds.

He set up in Cavendish Square and waited for orders. At the beginning he had a pretty lean time, but a commission for a portrait from the Duke of Richmond set him on the highroad to success. After that there was no looking back.

"A Lady and Child" was painted about 1782. The figures are pleasantly placed on the canvas. It is an honest piece of work devoid of any distinction of manner. The subject is one which is naturally attractive, and as the artist has set down very carefully what he saw, we accept it as such without being specially interested to know what he felt.

PLATE 72.—A LADY AND CHILD: Romney.

PLATE 73.—GEORGE ROMNEY (1734-1802)

"THE PARSON'S DAUGHTER"

ROMNEY'S chief title to fame is the large assortment of portraits of attractive young women which he has bequeathed to posterity. It was in 1782 that he first met the "Divine Emma," afterwards celebrated as Lady Hamilton. She proved an inspiring and versatile model. In all, he painted about forty portraits of her. She appeared in 1784 in his "Lady Hamilton as a Bacchante leading a Goat." That was not her only rôle. We see her in rapid succession as Ariadne, Calypso, Cassandra, Circe, *et hoc genus omne*, never to speak of St. Joan of Arc, Mary Magdalene, Nature, a Nun, St. Cecilia, and Sensibility. One wonders how the poor woman found time for all the sittings.

She is not, however, "The Parson's Daughter" of our illustration. That honour, in all probability, attaches to Mrs. Mark Currie, the wife of a banker resident in Surrey. It is a pleasant picture of English maidenhood in the best rectory lawn tradition. It has indeed an undeniable charm, and will never be without its admirers. But it illustrates Romney's defects as well as his qualities. It is too sweetly pretty. He never goes below the surface of things. He is ready to sacrifice everything for the sake of a superficial attraction. One looks in vain for any evidence of deep emotion, for any real passion in his work, and where that is lacking greatness is inevitably lacking too.

PLATE 73.—THE PARSON'S DAUGHTER: Romney.

PLATE 74.—SIR H. RAEBURN (1756–1823)

"PORTRAIT OF MRS. LAUZUN"

RAEBURN was a Scotsman and spent most of his life in Edinburgh. This may account for the fact that he has not been more prominently identified with our classical school of eighteenth-century portraiture. To his more fashionable contemporaries he doubtless appeared somewhat of a provincial, but when one comes to examine his work, one finds that it is certainly superior to Romney's, and although lacking the exquisite charm of Gainsborough's, can in many respects hold its own with the best of Reynolds's.

Like the others, his talents revealed themselves at an early age. He was apprenticed to a goldsmith in his native city, and rapidly acquired a reputation as a painter of miniatures. In 1778 he made a romantic marriage. A young widow, Ann Leslie by name, of gentle birth as well as of considerable fortune, "presented herself at his studio and desired to sit for her portrait." Within a month's time they were man and wife. They spent two years together in Italy, where it is to be feared his good Presbyterian upbringing did not take too kindly to Roman religious art. It was possibly all for the best. Returning to Edinburgh in 1787, he established himself as a portrait painter, and was soon inundated by commissions from "the aristocracy and intellect of Scotland."

He evolved a style which was admirably suited for coping with such, and which at the same time afforded an adequate expression of his own robust personality. It had, above all things, a masculine honesty expressed in "square fluent brushwork." This gave it a certain strength, and even ruggedness, which was reinforced by his simple and direct use of colour.

As might be expected, his most characteristic work is to be seen in Edinburgh, but this portrait of Mrs. Lauzun is an excellent example of his art. It has none of the elusive lightness of Gainsborough. It is much more downright, and reveals the breadth and freedom of his handling. The face is the important thing in this picture. Raeburn is not much interested in the subtleties of feminine attire, but he obviously took a delight in the delicately coloured glimpse of landscape seen to the right under the heavily filled-in shade of the tree that serves as a background.

His pictures have aged well. They are almost as fresh as when he painted them, a thing which cannot be said of Sir Joshua Reynolds.

He was knighted in 1822. A year later he died, leaving behind him an achievement that places him in the forefront of Scottish art, and sets him beside the most famous of English portrait painters.

PLATE 74.—PORTRAIT OF MRS. LAUZUN: Raeburn.

PLATE 75.—GEORGE MORLAND (1763–1804)

"THE INSIDE OF A STABLE"

IT is strange that the famous school of eighteenth-century English portrait painting does not seem to have contained within itself the seeds of future growth. It rose and flourished, gave to the world the exquisite flowering of Gainsborough's genius, and then as suddenly declined. Sir Thomas Lawrence's work only reveals a diminution of power. It prolongs but does not add to the tradition. Landscape painting was to become increasingly the field for English invention, but before we pass on, we may stop to consider the beginnings of a peculiarly national type of genre picture, those studies of animals and sporting pieces which are a recurrent phenomenon in British art.

George Stubbs (1724–1806) may be said to have started the fashion. His "Landscape: with a Gentleman holding his Horse" (No. 1452 in the Tate Gallery) is the founder of a long pedigree whose thoroughbreds delight us to-day in the equestrian paintings of Mr. Alfred Munnings. George Morland is of the same lineage. His father, Henry Morland, was a gifted portrait painter, but it was his reckless and dissipated son who raised the family name to its position in English art.

One can detect a certain amount of Dutch influence in his work, but he learnt more from the genre pictures of Hogarth. The alehouse and the farmyard provided him with the subjects most congenial to his disposition. Many have gone farther and fared worse. He was not, however, a realist. He inherited, possibly from his father, an inclination towards a somewhat conventional prettiness. It has been said of him that "his pigsties are as æsthetic as the drawing-room pieces of Lancret."

This stable scene has none of the reek of the barndoor. It is the sort of picture that is selected for Christmas cards and calendars, because of its pleasing and romantic intimacy. It is not a great work. He can be seen to better advantage in his "Reckoning" at the Victoria and Albert Museum. But it does illustrate the facility with which he painted horses, and the delicacy of his brushwork, and naturalistic use of colour. These qualities, together with his love for homely truth, have endeared him to a large public, and make one regret a career of such promise cut short by a dissolute and untimely end.

PLATE 75.—THE INSIDE OF A STABLE : Morland.

PLATE 76.—GAINSBOROUGH (1727–1788)

"THE MARKET CART"

GAINSBOROUGH is remembered chiefly as a portrait painter, but he did not confine his talents wholly to that branch of art. Among his earliest works are several studies in landscape, and although he did not pursue it as his life-work, he could, when he chose, transfer the lightness of his brush to the painting of trees no less than lissome ladies, and to the composition of pleasant rustic scenes as well as family groups and conversation pieces.

He has been alternately hailed as the forerunner of Constable and as the uninspired conventionalist. Both views are wide of the mark. It is true that he was not a startling innovator, but his "feathery" trees have a lightness that is no mere borrowed plumage. They have a grace of their own, and sometimes in their russet depths, in their intricate arabesques of shade, we get a foretaste of the glimpses that were to be revealed to us by the later and more naturalistic schools.

"The Market Cart" is a typical example of his landscape painting. It will be at once noticed that the prevailing colour is a rich brown. This was the convention of his age. It was not the fashion to look at nature directly. Style was formed by a study of the old masters, and as many of their canvases had acquired a tawny patina, often due, in fact, to the fading of their colours, this autumnal hue was considered the correct dress, even for the foliage of spring.

So, although these trees are in full leaf, there is not a single passage of green in this picture. A grey horse drawing a cart is plodding into a small pool. Two boys with a dog are conducting the equipage, and in the foreground, to the left, are two children. Under the tree, on the right, a youth with a red cape is collecting a bundle of faggots. The trees are painted with a deft touch. Despite the prevailing sepia, there is a pleasing gradation of light and shade.

We feel an affection for this picture without being particularly moved by it. Gainsborough has done what he set out to do very competently. To have attempted more would have seemed beside the point to his generation; and at any rate, by his very acceptance of the current conventionality, he avoided the pitfalls of tedious realism, and produced a work which, whatever may be its limitations, is a work of art.

PLATE 76.—THE MARKET CART: Gainsborough.

PLATE 77.—JOHN CROME (1768–1821)

"THE WINDMILL ON MOUSEHOLD HEATH"

JOHN CROME, the founder of the famous Norwich School, was born in that city in a small public house kept by his father, who combined the business of landlord with that of a journeyman weaver. At the age of fifteen he was apprenticed to a coach and sign painter, and used to spend his spare time in making sketches of the landscape in the vicinity of Norwich.

Crome, who is often referred to as Old Crome to distinguish him from his son (also a painter), occupies an intermediate place in the history of English landscape. He represents an advance towards naturalism when compared with Gainsborough or the typical eighteenth-century classicists, but he had not yet attained the freedom of Constable (his contemporary), with whom the modern conception of landscape painting may be said to begin. Crome's masters were the Dutch. He had an immense admiration for Hobbema, whose "Avenue at Middelharnis" we have illustrated (Plate 63). On his deathbed he is reported to have said: "Hobbema, my dear Hobbema, how I have loved you." Fortunately he was no mere plagiarist. He had a mind of his own, a sensitivity towards a certain type of beauty to which he gave full play.

This picture, "The Windmill on Mousehold Heath," which in his own words he painted "for the sake of air and space," reveals very clearly how fully he realized his objective. A golden light seems to distil from the sky, touching the soft green outline of the hill, and filling the atmosphere with its suffused glow. In the foreground a man on a small pony is riding through a gateway past a signpost. The track he is following leads up the rise to the windmill on the crest. Two donkeys are grazing on the edge of a gravel-pit hollowed in the flank of the hill. The sky is soft and autumnal in its serenity.

It will be noticed that for all his luminosity and width of atmosphere he has not shaken off the shackles of the "brown" school. The trees are brown, and so is much of the foreground. It was the convention of his time, and not until Constable came on to the scene was it to be dispensed with. Crome, however, was already well on the path that was to lead English landscape painting to its most notable achievements.

77

PLATE 77.—THE WINDMILL ON MOUSEHOLD HEATH: Crome.

PLATE 78.—J. CONSTABLE (1776–1837)

"FLATFORD MILL, ON THE RIVER STOUR"

THE sources of English landscape painting are not difficult to trace. The art of Claude Lorrain had begun to make its influence felt, especially in the work of Richard Wilson (1714–1782), and at a later date Turner was to find inspiration for his earlier studies in the work of the great French master. Claude was a painter of transition. His compositions are classical in their conception. It was still felt that no landscape was complete without the addition of some architectural detail, ruined temples or palaces in the Græco-Roman style, their columns and architraves carefully disposed to invest the scene with a dignity which was considered lacking in nature itself. Similarly groups of figures might be introduced to lend a human or mythological interest, and endow the picture with a title more in keeping with prevalent fashion.

But already Claude had begun to be enamoured of the atmospheric effects of nature itself. His love of sunlight flooding vast vistas with its glow, his delight in aerial perspective wherein the distance takes on the loveliness of a mirage, proclaim him as one of the founders of modern landscape painting. (Turner's " Crossing the Brook," Plate 83, exhibits many of these qualities.)

The other influence came from Holland, and is evident, as we have noted, in the works of the Norwich School. But neither Crome nor Gainsborough (whose " Market Cart " has been illustrated) had broken away from the tradition that required a certain conventionality in the composition, and was inclined to look at nature through brown-tinted spectacles. This preference for russet tones, born of a conservative respect for the tarnished canvases of the older masters, was, like Charles II., an unconscionably long time in dying. It was left for Constable to give it its final dispatch. For the first time the vivid green of nature invaded the domain of landscape painting.

" Flatford Mill, on the river Stour," painted in 1817, shows that even then he had developed a style that was conspicuous for its intimate naturalism. He had brought painting out of doors.

The scene is typically English. In the near foreground a horse with a boy on its back is being attached to the towing rope of a barge floating idly on the stream. In the distance is a lock and the buildings of the mill. To the right of the picture stretches a level expanse of pasture, interspersed with trees. The time is early summer, when the foliage is heaviest and the grass has not lost the freshness of spring. Green shadows dapple the sunlit sward, and over all is a soft and tranquil sky.

Out of such subject matter Constable was to build his art, and the next two plates show how it grew in maturity and power.

PLATE 78.—FLATFORD MILL : Constable.

PLATE 79.—J. CONSTABLE (1776–1837)

"THE HAY WAIN"

CONSTABLE had been born, the son of a well-to-do miller, at East Bergholt in Suffolk, and that pleasant region of East Anglia was to be the cradle of his art. As early as 1802 he writes, " For the last two years I have been running after pictures and seeking the truth at second hand. I shall return to Bergholt, where I shall endeavour to get a pure and unaffected manner of representing the scenes that may employ me. There is room for a natural painter."

His early works had not excited any marked attention, but suddenly in 1824, he sprang into fame with " The Hay Wain," which was exhibited in the Paris Salon of that year. Looking at this homely and nowadays almost old-fashioned picture, it is perhaps hard for us to realize the sensation it caused when it first caught the public's eye. It was from the French he received his first chorus of praise. One eminent critic said of his work, " You can see the dew on the blades of grass," and the great Delacroix himself remarked, " He is the father of our school of landscape." To understand the furore which this picture excited it is necessary to bear in mind how singular a departure it was from the accepted conventions of landscape painting. The " brown " school was still in the ascendancy. Sir George Beaumont, one of his patrons, recommended Constable to make the colour of an old Cremona fiddle the dominating note of his canvases, whereupon Constable by way of retort laid a violin on the green lawn before the house. On another occasion on being asked, " Do you find it very difficult to determine where to place your ' brown tree ' ? " he replied, " Not in the least. I never put such a thing into my pictures." There is no " brown tree " in " The Hay Wain." Instead the foliage is painted a transparently limpid green, the pure luminous colour of leaves after rain, for in this picture Constable has painted the weather quite as much as the scene itself. Although the moment chosen is one of fitful sunshine, it has been a day of showers, and their freshness still sparkles on the grass and the clump of oak trees. In the foreground a wain is fording a shallow stream, swollen by the recent downpour. By a punt on the right a man is fishing. A contrast to the prevailing green is provided by the tiled roof of the cottage on the left, and the bright touch of red on the harness of the horses.

He has set it down with directness and freshness of vision, and so unusual were these qualities at the time that it is not surprising this very picture is now generally regarded by European critics to be the point of departure of the Barbizon School of 1830 and of the whole of modern landscape painting.

PLATE 79.—THE HAY WAIN : Constable.

PLATE 80.—J. CONSTABLE (1776–1837)

"A CORNFIELD WITH FIGURES"
Tate Gallery

THE other Constables illustrated have for their prevailing colour his fresh and inimitable handling of greens. This early sketch—our sole example from the Tate Gallery—is interesting as showing his happy use of golden browns and reds. The execution is more rapid than that of either " Flatford Mill " or " The Hay Wain," and points the way to the extreme freedom he was to acquire in later works such as our next plate.

Little analysis is necessary. The figures are disposed very effectively, without any studied elaboration. They add just the touch of human activity that the harvest scene requires. The gold of the cornfield heightens by contrast the cloudy greens of the towering elm and other trees.

Once again we are conscious of being in the open air, and of Constable's direct and vivid delight in nature. He is the Wordsworth of English painters. There could not be any better epitome of a peculiarly English aspect of art than an edition of the *Lyrical Ballads* with illustrations by Constable.

PLATE 80.—A CORNFIELD WITH FIGURES: Constable.

PLATE 81.—J. CONSTABLE (1776–1837)

"SALISBURY CATHEDRAL"

NO work of art ever resulted from the mere transcription or copying of nature; for art involves the personality of the artist, and is strong or weak in proportion to his depth of feeling and insight. Its roots are in a passion-ate apprehension of visual form, and the combination of those forms, be they lines, or masses, or colours, capable of evoking the emotion experienced by the artist when he set himself to create. That is the gist of the problem as it presents itself to him, but there is no hard and fast rule for its working out. It is not a mere question of skill in the handling of paint—many negligible artists have acquired a technical facility—it is rather the discovery of the particular manner or mode of expression best suited to be the vehicle of his vision. He can learn much from the masters who have preceded him, but the final adjustment of his medium to his own personal sensibility is a matter that he must settle for himself. Out of this process, often quite in-stinctive (as in the case of Gainsborough and Van Gogh), sometimes deliberately conscious in its empiricism, comes the achievement of style. For in painting, no less than in the other arts, one can say with reason, " le style, c'est l'homme."

The repetition of these platitudes is suggested by " Salisbury Cathedral," painted by Constable in his later period. Its style is highly conscious and individualistic. More than ever he is concerned with a vivid apprehension of nature, seen under all the changing aspects our fickle weather imposes upon it. But experience has made him more daring, and in this picture he has caught an almost ferocious intensity, one of those lightning moods when an overcast sky flings down on spire and roof and straining tree its passing shadow and its equally fleeting violence of light.

To achieve this he has used a technique in which his pigment is as tortured as the gusts of thundery air. The execution is so rapid as to seem almost careless in its audacity. A great part of the enjoy-ment derived from this picture comes from Constable's handling of the actual paint, especially in his brilliant use of impasto.

This is indeed an Impressionist painting, and marks him definitely as an innovator. Later we shall have to go into the question more fully. Our last plate, Van Gogh's " Landscape with Cypress Trees," reveals the same excitement of feeling in his case, of consuming heat and sun-shine, as in this picture of the sultry grey-blue intensity of rain.

PLATE 81.—SALISBURY CATHEDRAL : Constable.

PLATE 82.—J. M. W. TURNER (1775–1851)

"CALAIS PIER"

TURNER in all probability was the most imaginative artist England has ever produced. He was born on April 23, 1775, at the house of his father, who was a barber in Covent Garden. His talent disclosed itself early, for at the age of ten he had begun to draw. He was apprenticed to Thomas Malton, the architectural draughtsman, the task entrusted to him being that of colouring his master's engravings. We possess in his pictures a remarkably succinct history of his life; for the liberality of his will left to the nation a bequest that is unequalled both in its generosity and in the way in which it reveals the development of a genius, not a little eccentric in its attachments, but singularly unanimous in its quest of self-expression.

An islander born and bred, he was the first to reveal to his fellow islanders the beauty of the sea. He had far passed his apprenticeship when he produced the " Calais Pier," illustrated on the opposite page. Possibly it owes a little to the Dutch masters, but it is informed with a vigour that is quite its own. French fishing-boats are putting out to a not too friendly sea, and athwart them the English packet under brown sails is entering the harbour. In the foreground a magnificent curl of wave, crisped like a shell, portrays the conflict of wind and tide. The pier is crowded with figures, noticeable among whom is a woman in a red dress, who appears to be gesticulating to a fisherman in the boat below.

A storm would seem to be either brewing or disintegrating, and from its murky violence the lighting of the picture is derived. It is no mere studio effect. No less than Constable he has gone out of doors. In appearance he was somewhat of a bluff old salt, and one likes to think that it was his sea-eye which observed the white and angry line of foam along the horizon. An unrigged ship beating up the Channel adds to the vivid atmospheric effect.

For all its bustle and episodic animation this picture confines and delights the eye within the limit of its compass. This is evidence of its unity of composition. Its vitality needs no commendation. The colouring is masterful. A sombre harmony holds together all the varying and shifting sources of light.

Those who, like the writer, are aware of the salt in their veins, will always be attracted by the seascapes of Turner.

PLATE 82.—CALAIS PIER: Turner.

PLATE 83.—J. M. W. TURNER (1775–1851)

"CROSSING THE BROOK"

THIS lovely picture reveals another aspect of Turner's genius. No great artist is completely isolated. However idiosyncratic he may be, he owes a debt to his predecessors. It is only the fool who disclaims them. Turner went abroad on the "Grand Tour," but even had he stayed at home his inquisitive mind would have delved into the traditions that had gone to the moulding of landscape art. In this work he is undoubtedly indebted to Richard Wilson, and through him to Claude Lorrain. That great French master was one of the founders of modern landscape. As we have mentioned, his convention demanded the inclusion of idyllic figures in the foreground, and of architectural features, ruined temples it might be, ingeniously disposed so as to invest the accidents of nature with the civilizing presence of man.

And so in this picture, which is a view of the Tamar looking towards Plymouth from Calstock, we have a bare-legged girl about to ford the river, calling to a dog in mid-stream, while another nymph, in a light blue dress, sits on the right-hand bank. In the middle distance a bridge crosses the valley with all the archæological rectitude of a Roman aqueduct. The pine on the left, with a little imagination, might almost be a stone pine, the familiar shade of a Mediterranean landscape, sister of the pine in his lovely "Golden Bough" in the Dublin Gallery.

Such harmonies had been used by other painters, but few before him had carried aerial perspective to such an infinitude of recession. The vivid detail of the foreground only exists as a foil to its vast expanse.

We are conscious of being on a height and untroubled by any vicissitude of weather, of seeing the landscape dream itself into the distance, idealized it may be, but none the less compelling. The balancing of the dark masses of foliage emphasizes the dip of the valley, and the quiet, undramatic lighting sacrifices nothing of the luminosity we might expect under such a tranquil sky, illuminating with its soft radiance a landscape viewed from such a high and romantic point of vantage.

PLATE 83.—CROSSING THE BROOK: Turner.

PLATE 84.—J. M. W. TURNER (1775–1851)

" THE EVENING STAR "
Tate Gallery

THIS exceedingly beautiful painting represents the art of Turner at its purest and most serene. Its appeal is so compelling that any analysis seems unnecessary. No one has ever surpassed Turner in his ability to capture the mood of a scene, to set down the evanescent effects of light and shadow in all their subtlety.

He has chosen here one of those moments when land and sea and sky take on a loveliness that is doubly poignant because of its transience. The sun has just gone down behind a bank of sombre cloud, tinging its edges with a miraculous orange glow. The wide expanse of sky is suffused with its luminosity, and faintly silver soars in mid-air the star that gives the picture its name. Nor in air only, for a higher spot of light mirrors its image on the dark merge of wave and wave-wet shore.

The scene is one of solitude, its very loneliness being heightened by the fisher boy and his dog, wending their way home in the darkening light. The sparse and ghost-like sails of a ship add to the mystery.

It is a moment of exquisite tranquillity, and over all is that air of sadness inseparable from such a mood.

The greatness of this picture arises from the compelling way in which Turner has made us share his emotion. We see the scene through his eyes, and go away richer for the experience. One cannot ask more of any work of art.

PLATE 84.—THE EVENING STAR : Turner.

PLATE 85.—J. M. W. TURNER (1775–1851)

"ULYSSES DERIDING POLYPHEMUS"

IT has been said of Turner that he suffered from a too active imagination. There is truth in the remark. All through his life he was haunted by dreams verging on the grandiose and the impossible. We may be thankful that he was never ensnared by the literary realism which was to be the grave of the pre-Raphaelites, but it would have been better for posterity had he escaped the glamorous allure that mythology, heightened by the achievement of certain romantic painters, offered to his eyes. About the same time that he painted "The Evening Star" he indulged his fantasy in this, possibly the most successful of his grandiloquent paintings.

On the shore, in the left-hand corner of the picture, is seen the glow of the smouldering fire in which Ulysses heated the staff with which he gouged out the eye of Polyphemus. The monster sprawls his ungainly bulk on the top of the cliff, dissolving into the forms of the clouds. To the centre, left, the magnificent galley of Ulysses, its deck and masts crowded with men, is getting under way on its voyage home, while on the right the sun is setting between a caverned rock and a flotilla of glowing ships. These are the incidents. They provide a dangerous seduction, and between the Scylla and Charybdis of mythology and realism Turner has sailed not an altogether unperilous course.

We may presume he was preoccupied with the legend, but in truth the charm of this picture consists in his painting of light. Its orange glow is manifest everywhere, on the wine-coloured Homeric sea, on the sails of the ships, and the miraculous sky. But this richness of colouring and of epic content is not a substitute for strictness of design, or for the magic that is to be found in the imaginative handling of actual things.

The picture remains slightly rhetorical, slightly unreal, and a warning to lesser painters—and indeed to himself—that fantasy has its dangers, and wears less well than the immediate apprehension of reality.

PLATE 85.—ULYSSES DERIDING POLYPHEMUS: Turner.

PLATE 86.—J. M. W. TURNER (1775–1851)

"HASTINGS"
Tate Gallery

BEFORE we proceed to an analysis of the next two Turners, we would do well to attempt a definition, in so far as it is to be defined, of Impressionism. For between himself and Constable (*vide* Salisbury Cathedral, Plate 81) they had arrived at the Impressionistic formula. To a later generation Impressionism was to present itself as an escape from photographic realism. That bugbear had not descended upon earlier painters, and the most minute of the miniaturists, the most realistic of the Dutch genre painters, could claim at the lowest that they were doing something that could not be done otherwise. Usually they managed to do much more.

All art is a species of evocation. As such it cannot repeat itself without disaster. The condition of vitality is innovation. One of the features of classical art had been a sculpturesque definition, which concerned itself primarily with figure and subject painting. Landscape on the whole had been relegated to a subordinate position. When it began to engage men's minds with an intrinsic value of its own, they were brought face to face with the fact that it was not amenable to studio conditions. It changed. It was influenced above all things by light. Conventional Impressionism set out to paint light, and its preoccupation with the spectrum was the most fundamental tenet of its creed.

But it did much more. Evocation can be provoked by suggestion as well as by statement. The elusive can stimulate. Its vagueness of definition, its nuance of forms seen under the varying conditions of atmosphere, can produce a mood all the more arresting because the eye is not troubled by the presence of photographic detail.

And so in this picture of the beach at Hastings Turner is only concerned with the broadest of effects. The orange sail of the stranded boat serves to focus the eye, but it is not what he was primarily interested in. He is setting down rapidly and sketchily an aspect of light, as it touches the sea and veils the cliffs in a luminous haze. The foreground is a vague miasma, almost a mirror for the changing sky.

Claude Monet, one of the founders of the French Impressionistic School, some decades later, was to declare : " The light is the real person in the picture." His words are the best comment on this canvas.

PLATE 86.—HASTINGS: Turner.

PLATE 87.—J. M. W. TURNER (1775–1851)

" RAIN, STEAM, AND SPEED "

THE title of this picture is the best indication of the intention in Turner's mind when he set his hand to this canvas. Painted in 1843 it is his last great work, for the closing years of his life were to witness a diminution of his powers. His vision became confused, his handling less and less certain. Even in this picture the dissolution had begun.

One critic has described it as " the first and greatest attempt to elicit beauty out of a railway train." In 1843 trains were considered ugly. Ruskin, who idolized Turner, thought them an abomination. To introduce such a subject into polite art was to fly in the face of all convention. The progress of poetry affords a similar parallel. Conservatism for a long time considered the vocabulary of modern technology as unpoetic. To many timid souls it is still outside the pale of " literary " usage.

But Turner indeed was not painting a train. He was painting an impression of steam and speed, and is so little concerned with the obvious that he has placed the fire on front of the engine, instead of in the fire-box. The long perspective of the viaduct is merely a device for giving direction to the impetus he wishes to portray. He has reduced everything to a tenuous and symbolic suggestion. Rapidity of execution, absence of definition, the chaos of the elements dissolving the forms of landscape in the solvent of wind and rain, these were the means he used, these the effects he sought.

The picture leaves a vivid impression, but we remember it as we remember a dream. By a curious paradox he has used the very real forces of rain and steam and speed to produce what is almost an abstraction. Such a process may be interesting and arresting, but the vagueness of the design, the licence he permits himself in the handling of purely atmospheric effects, can be carried too far, can become too insubstantial. And this picture is a border-line case.

The intensity of his imaginative vision ended by defeating itself, and his final years of declining strength produced no works of lasting importance.

He died on December 19, 1851, and was laid to rest beside Sir Joshua Reynolds in the crypt of St. Paul's.

PLATE 87.—RAIN, STEAM, AND SPEED : Turner.

PLATE 88.—GABRIEL DANTE ROSSETTI (1828–1882)

"BEATA BEATRIX"
Tate Gallery

NOTWITHSTANDING the examples of Constable and Turner, English art at the middle of the nineteenth century had reached a pretty low ebb. Turner was too personal both in his vision and in his methods to have any immediate influence other than a dangerous one. Constable, as we have noted, was assimilated more readily by the French. Painting in England inclined more and more to be dominated by literary and anecdotal interests. Every picture told a story, and the story was usually accounted of greater importance than the picture. Affected sentiment both in subject matter and in style was the note of the age.

In 1848 three young men banded themselves together in an attempt to find a way out. They were Rossetti, Holman Hunt, and Millais. They called the society they founded the pre-Raphaelite Brotherhood. Foremost among their aims was a strict study of natural detail and effect, and in their pursuit of purity of style they looked back to the pre-Renaissance Italian masters, very much as a Tractarian Churchman of the time found a rest for his soul in the Early Fathers. How far their practice matched their creed is a debatable matter. The whole movement, if precise in name, was somewhat nebulous in its results. It was certainly not a return to nature in the sense that either Constable or the Impressionists would have understood it. And they did not shake off the literary influence; in fact, they intensified it. The most that one can say is that they substituted the poetic for the prosaic as a source of pictorial inspiration.

Rossetti himself was a poet before anything else. Such a subject as Beata Beatrix could be better expressed in poetry than in paint.

Dante's divine lady in a plum-coloured robe and bright green tunic is seated on a balcony with a sundial on the parapet. In the distance is a bridge across the Arno. It was painted by Rossetti in memory of the death of his wife, whose features he has given to Beatrix. " This picture is not intended at all to represent death," he writes, " but to render it under the semblance of a trance in which Beatrix is suddenly rapt from earth to heaven."

The theme was so near his heart that, in spite of the straining after poetic abstraction, Rossetti has succeeded in conveying his emotion.

PLATE 88.—BEATA BEATRIX: Rossetti.

PLATE 89.—SIR EDWARD BURNE-JONES (1833–1898)

"KING COPHETUA AND THE BEGGAR MAID"
Tate Gallery

WE have noted that one of the tendencies of the pre-Raphaelite movement was to exalt the conception that the more remote and idealistic the subject of a picture, the greater value it was likely to possess as a work of art. Nothing could be more misleading. The sublimity or otherwise of its theme has little to do with a picture's greatness. In England especially, where literary associations have led so many painters astray, it was a doctrine of peculiar danger, one that needed to be suppressed rather than encouraged.

This predilection for romanticism often went hand-in-hand with an attitude towards life that was one of retreat. Unable to create beauty out of an immediate apprehension of reality, the artist withdrew into a world of his own poetic imagining. This bloodless negation, this denial and rejection of the conditions which can alone produce vitality, is writ large over the works of Burne-Jones. He is at his best when he is a decorator, making designs for tapestries or stained glass, for in such work the necessity of complying with technical conventions helps to hide his inherent timidity, which is only too evident when he is faced with the freedom afforded by either pencil or brush.

" King Cophetua and the Beggar Maid " shows at once both the qualities and defects of his essentially limited genius. It is a purely decorative work, full of an exquisite handling of minute detail, but devoid of any single compelling purpose. Its design falters. There is no rhythmic feeling in its composition, no focus of interest or climax of emotion. The king, seated at the feet of the beggar maid, is scarcely more important than the background. The relationship of the complicated planes of the picture has no significance. In so far as any exists, it is quite fortuitous. Quite the most charming passage in this work is that of the two youths, their heads inclined to each other, bending over an illuminated score from which they are singing.

One can trace influences from as distant sources as Botticelli and Crivelli. Lost in a picturesque and sentimentalized mediævalism, he seems deliberately to have turned his back upon the world of reality. And so his work exists in a kind of vacuum, " a survival of an attractive but retrograde, and perhaps somewhat morbid, love of the past."

PLATE 89.—KING COPHETUA AND THE BEGGAR MAID: Burne-Jones.

PLATE 90.—SIR GEORGE CLAUSEN (1852-1944)

"THE GIRL AT THE GATE"
Tate Gallery

THE most significant developments in the history of painting during the nineteenth century took place in France. England can claim to have had her finger in the pie at the beginnings of the famous Barbizon School, for it was Constable's "Hay Wain" (Plate 79), exhibited at the Salon of 1824, that pointed the way to that return to nature which was one of the chief characteristics of the new movement.

Not less important was the influence of Corot, towards lyricism, and of Courbet, towards realism in the treatment of subject matter. The Barbizon School comprised such well-known artists as Daubigny, Diaz, and Millet, all more united in their spirit of approach towards nature than in any doctrinary discipline or similarity of style. Crumbs from their table began to fall in England in the later Victorian period. With them must be included Bastien-Lepage, whose naturalism offered a plainer and more wholesome fare than the elaborate recipes of the pre-Raphaelites, and as such had a beneficial if not profoundly exciting stimulus.

In this picture Sir George Clausen is considerably indebted to Bastien-Lepage. It is not a great work, but at least it is a satisfactory one, painted with a transparent honesty, and quite a deal of psychological insight.

The girl at once attracts our attention by her simple, unstudied attitude and directness of expression. The artist was obviously interested in her, and has set down very compellingly the look of anxiety that is in her face. The background is pleasantly painted with a feeling of real naturalism that is an agreeable relief after the sophistication and academic insipidity that still marred so much contemporary work. Possibly it is weakened just a little by a slight trace of sentimentality. Sincerity is a good beginning, but it is not enough, and Sir George Clausen's later work (this was painted in 1889) possesses greater vitality without sacrificing anything of the directness that gives this picture its appeal.

PLATE 90.—THE GIRL AT THE GATE: Clausen.

PLATE 91.—P. WILSON STEER

"PAINSWICK BEACON"
Tate Gallery

THE inauguration of the New English Art Club in 1886 is a more important date in the history of British painting than that which saw the founding of the pre-Raphaelite Brotherhood. From the outset the pre-Raphaelite movement suffered from a pedantic self-consciousness, and its literary idealism deflected painting from its true orientation. The New English Art Club set out with no cut-and-dry formula. It was revolutionary only in the sense that it stood for freedom of expression. And it provided a place where artists who were unrecognized by the Academy or antagonistic to its spirit could exhibit their work.

It is hard to realize the position of art as it was in the eighteen-eighties. The Royal Academy, by reason of its endowments and vested interests, was the most powerful, and indeed the only, body of its kind in the country. It was essentially conservative and hide-bound. Public taste was at a deplorably low level, and the new artists had to make their way in the face both of official disapprobation and general apathy. Their first exhibitions included artists of such varied talent and outlook as Clausen, Mark Fisher, Lavery, Shannon, Tuke, and Wilson Steer. As a group they were fully aware of the importance of the French Impressionist School. Indeed at first it was intended to limit membership to artists who had studied in France. Anything rather than the dull and lifeless mediocrity of the Academic schools.

Wilson Steer was one of the original members of the group. He was strongly under the influence of the Impressionists, but he was equally conscious of the English examples of Constable and Turner. "Painswick Beacon" is essentially an English picture. One makes that statement, and immediately one is aware that it would be difficult to define what is implied by it. The landscape is English, so is the weather, but one feels that these would have been seen differently by, say, a French painter. Is it true that as a race we are less conscious of style in the abstract, less doctrinaire in our self-expression? And does the word "freedom"—another dangerously ambiguous term—suggest any meaning in this connection? The freshness of handling, so noticeable in Hogarth's "Shrimp Girl" (Plate 66), is apparent in this picture. In both there is a happy absence of restraint. Wilson Steer's highly personal art—and he is a painter of many moods and aspects—seems at any rate more natively English than, for example, that of his brilliant contemporary, Richard Sickert. And when we use the word English, we are thinking only of the best.

PLATE 91.—PAINSWICK BEACON: Steer.

PLATE 92.—SIR WILLIAM ORPEN (1878–1931)

"THE MIRROR"
Tate Gallery

SIR WILLIAM ORPEN captured the public eye largely through the brilliancy of his portraiture. He had an innate sense of style, and evolved a highly personal technique, rapid, incisive, and sparkling in its virtuosity. His handling of paint is always interesting. There is hardly a dull square foot in one of his pictures. He could make a khaki tunic, a morning coat, or a surgeon's red rubber gloves look exciting, and this superficial dexterity was backed up by sound draughtsmanship and a penetrating flair for characterization. The secret of his method seems to lie in the glittering quality he gave to his high lights, and in his crisp and sharp use of half-tones, flicked on to the canvas with an unerring accuracy. It ended by becoming a mannerism, almost a formula even. People who were fortunate enough to be able to commission a portrait from his hands, or whose friends sought to honour them by so doing, knew pretty well beforehand what they would get. He might not flatter them, but at any rate he would make them look interesting.

These qualities were a feature of his later work. They enabled him to carry through to a triumphant success such a *tour de force* as his well-known "Signing of the Peace Treaties at Versailles." But this facility had its dangers. Sometimes one suspects that it is just a little too slick, and that he lacked a certain depth of feeling.

"The Mirror" is an early work, and is hardly typical of the Orpen that dazzled the eye at so many exhibitions of the Academy. A girl is seated against a green wall with a yellow dado. She leans slightly forward, her hands on her knees, her feet on an olive-green footstool. She is wearing a white muslin blouse, and a black skirt draped with a grey shawl. Her face is shadowed by a hat trimmed with shot pink and brown ribbon, and a brown feather. The circular mirror reflects the artist at work at his easel, with the girl standing behind him.

It is a quiet picture, showing a pleasing command of colour and certainty of handling. The effect is a little heavy, and devoid of the animation one is accustomed to associate with his work.

Orpen was a Dublin man, and is one of the most distinguished artists Ireland has ever produced. The extent and variety of his work was well seen at the Commemorative Exhibition held at Burlington House in the winter of 1932–1933.

PLATE 92.—THE MIRROR: Orpen.

PLATE 93.—AUGUSTUS JOHN

"MADAME SUGGIA"
Tate Gallery

AUGUSTUS JOHN is a difficult person to define. You cannot pin him down or "formulate him in a phrase," as T. S. Eliot would say. He refuses to wear any labels. Call him a realist, and you are at once aware that he is a romanticist too. Call him the play-boy of contemporary painting (and certain aspects of his high spirited and exuberant genius seems to justify the epithet), and immediately you are face to face with the fact that he is an intensely serious artist. The simplest thing is just to say that he is great, and to leave it at that. He knows how to draw—knows it supremely well—and he knows how to paint.

It is a pity that we are unable to reproduce his "Smiling Woman." It antedates this portrait by some thirteen years, and has been on view at the Tate Gallery since 1917. It wears well. It possesses a greater concentration and, although less immediately striking, emanates a strangely haunting loveliness that lingers in the mind. But indeed both works are not easily forgotten.

Those who have been privileged to hear Madame Suggia's playing, and to see her on the concert platform, where her magnificent poise seems but another aspect of her musicianship, will have no hesitation in realizing how fully Augustus John has caught the spirit of his distinguished sitter. This portrait strikes a note of verve. The ease and absolute certitude of the long and shapely arm, with the nervous tension of the wrist and fingers as they grip the bow, is rendered with a skill that reflects John's mastery as forcibly as it does her own. Her crimson sweeping dress, with its extensive train deployed in the "grand manner," set against the folds of a green curtain relieved with yellowish lights, builds up a baroque pyramid, supporting at once the lady and her majestic instrument. It is interesting to note that the face is portrayed in a haughty profile.

This picture is clever, but it is more than that : it is supremely convincing. The quality of vitality here claims its own by an indubitable right, and where vitality is present, greatness is not far off.

PLATE 93.—MADAME SUGGIA: John.

PLATE 94.—RICHARD WALTER SICKERT (1860-1942)

"CAFÉ DES TRIBUNAUX, DIEPPE"
Tate Gallery

SICKERT with a singular integrity pursued his own course, following his genius where it led him, true at once to the French Impressionists who were his earliest mentors, and to his own individuality. One of the greatest of modern English painters, he is possibly the least in the national tradition. His spiritual home was Paris, or the Dieppe in which so many ex-patriot Englishmen have forgathered. One thinks of Ernest Dowson, of Wilde, for example, and even his latest work shows signs here and there of the ninetyish manner. That is not to say that it is in any way *démodé*. His exhibitions, and his all too meagre contributions to the walls of Burlington House, proved that he was keenly alive—the one native who could furnish a *sauce piquante* to spice the John Bullishness of our traditional diet.

This is comparatively an early work. Its direct honesty almost forbids an analysis. When one is asked to explain why it is a good painting, one is thrown back upon the rules which, if broken, lead to an inconsequence out of which nothing can be expected. It is at once formal and real. The heavy diagonal thrown by the shade in the foreground stops, where the brightest colours begin, under the awning of the café. Where its lethargy ends is the focus of interest, almost central indeed, though the effect is so natural as to appear one of accident rather than design.

Sickert was always an intriguing colourist. In this picture, as in so many of his works, he gets his effect, as one critic has very aptly said, "not so much by the use of pure colour as of colour seen in tones, by tone values rather than colour values." It is possibly a rather technical point, but it is worth noting, and suggests a clue to the undoubted colour subtlety of this work.

PLATE 94.—CAFÉ DES TRIBUNAUX, DIEPPE : Sickert.

PLATE 95.—EDOUARD MANET (1832–1883)
MODERN FRENCH SCHOOL

"LA SERVANTE DE BOCKS"
Tate Gallery

THE most important movements in modern painting have originated in France, and of these the most far-reaching in its influence has been that of Impressionism. It is not excessive to say that it has revolutionized our sense of colour values. Like all such innovations it was not an entirely new growth. There had been forerunners—our own Constable and Turner, as we have seen—who had brought painting out of doors and begun to study light in the way which was to become the conscious objective of the Impressionists. Painters like Corot, and the artists of the Barbizon School, paved the way for the advance. It was an age of great artistic activity in France, and new ideas were in the air. The modern attention paid to landscape-painting raised the problem of natural lighting and atmospheric effect. It was discovered that light was made up of primary colours. Impressionism brought the spectrum into the field of actual painting.

The artists who formed the nucleus of the new movement were Monet, Manet, Renoir, Sisley, and Pissarro. Monet and Pissarro were the two who adhered most strictly to the Impressionistic doctrine. They subordinated everything to the rendering of light, colour, and atmosphere, as seen at a given moment. Manet joined the group, not because he was primarily interested in their specific theories, but because he was in revolt against academic orthodoxy, which in France, as in England, was incredibly dull. His spiritual ancestor was Velazquez. Like him he knew how to create beautiful effects out of black, a colour which was afterwards banished from the Impressionist's palette. He has used it with effect in " La Servante de Bocks."

This can hardly be described as an Impressionist painting, though the effect of the movement can be seen in the vitality of his colour. Impressionism, in its preoccupation with the handling of light, was inclined to neglect drawing and design. Both these qualities Manet possessed in a high degree. He was one of the most naturally gifted artists who have ever lived. He could not paint anything without making it interesting. The trouble is that his genius was so omnivorous, and so talented in its expression, that at times we are aware of an uneasy suspicion that something is lacking—a profundity of mood perhaps, a depth of emotional contact with that life which he saw so brilliantly, and which only the greatest have dared to probe to the core.

PLATE 95.—LA SERVANTE DE BOCKS: Manet.

PLATE 96.—EDGAR DEGAS (1834-1917)
MODERN FRENCH SCHOOL

" FEMME ASSISE "
Tate Gallery

DEGAS exhibited with the Impressionists, but he was not of them in the narrower significance of the term. He had a command of subtle colouring, but it was his superb qualities as a draughtsman, and his highly personal sense of rhythm, that gave his art its distinction. He was intensely individual, both in his choice of subject matter and in his handling of it.

Impressionism has come to mean more than a preoccupation with the chromatic qualities of light. It implies a change of outlook. The artist did not seek to imitate nature in the dull representational manner of the academic schools, but to give us his own *impression* of reality. There was nothing inherently new in the idea, but it had never become so fully self-conscious. The artist's personality, his own intuitive reactions, were seen to be much more important to a work of art than mere choice of subject and facility of manipulation. This had been true from the beginning, but it now became an article of creed. That it brought with it an immense liberation cannot be denied. Personal idiom came into its own. Degas was one of the best equipped of the young painters to benefit from the new orientation.

With the passion that earlier masters had turned to religion for their themes, he turned to the world of the theatre, especially the theatre of the ballet. His studies of danseuses are probably the first things one associates with his name. Our superb " Miss Lola at the Cirque Fernando " shows what that exciting world could give him. The design is audacious. The problems of spatial relationships which he has set himself alone would make it unforgettable. And then what colour, what orange-reds, what pinks, what greens !

Portraiture he essayed less often, but this charming " Femme Assise " is full of his intimacy. He always painted his sitters against a background of their own personal surroundings, and, as in this picture, it plays an important part. He establishes at once a contact of sympathy with his subject, but he is reticent about it, and the reticence is shared almost equally between the girl in this picture and the artist. He keeps the secret of his style so much to himself that his work is full of subtle surprises. Even although we know that it is founded upon a highly conscious technique, he continually delights us by a note of improvisation, as it were, especially in his use of colour. His touches of scarlet in this picture, for example—had he seen their effect from the beginning, or were they added on the decision of a moment, a decision that is all the more convincing because it appears to be so spontaneous and so unforeseen ?

96

PLATE 96.—FEMME ASSISE: Degas.

PLATE 97.—PAUL CÉZANNE (1839-1906)
MODERN FRENCH SCHOOL

" CÉZANNE CHAUVE "
Tate Gallery

MORE has been written about Cézanne than about **any** modern painter. The buzz of discussion that surrounds his name has not abated yet, and is not likely to until some new planet swims into our ken, capable of suggesting so many problems to the astronomers, and of attracting such a number of satellites.

Paul Cézanne was born at Aix in Provence. He was largely self-taught. He painted with Pissarro, from whom he learnt much, but he soon saw the outstanding fault of Impressionism, its lack of solidity, its weakness of design. He studied in the Louvre, where he was specially attracted to the work of Rubens. He said he wished to make of Impressionist art something solid and enduring, " like the art of the museums." He realized that when painting forfeits the stimulus provided by volume, by three-dimensional form, it loses much of its power, and set himself quite deliberately to the task of restoring this to modern art. It had especially been overlooked in landscape-painting. Poussin, in all probability, was the last painter whose landscapes preserved this feeling of solidity, but to his methods, of course, there could be no return. What Massacio and Piero della Francesca did for early Florentine art in the achievement of " mass " in painting, Cézanne has done for our generation. They were concerned with figure compositions (so, indeed, was Cézanne), but Cézanne carried his discoveries into landscape and still life. His angular landscapes almost project from their frames. He seems to hew his shapes. And it is done by an entirely new technique. Colour, the vivid palette of the Impressionists, is the medium he uses to achieve this result. He splits his tones with an infinite subtlety, but they are never allowed to melt into each other. The outline is always sharp.

This portrait is typical of his arresting directness. It is painted in a low key, but within that range the eye will find innumerable gradations of tone.

Of Cézanne's influence on modern art we have not room to speak. His work has had a more wide-reaching effect than that of any recent painter. This is largely due to his intuitive grasp of form. He was not easily satisfied, and subjected himself to a severe discipline. The trouble is that many of his followers have been content to copy his mannerisms, without getting, as he invariably did, to the root of the matter.

PLATE 97.—CÉZANNE CHAUVE: Cézanne.

PLATE 98.—GEORGES SEURAT (1859-1891)
MODERN FRENCH SCHOOL

"LA BAIGNADE"
Tate Gallery

ONE very hot August afternoon I remember having gone down the Seine by steamer from Paris to St. Cloud. The banks were thronged with bathers, and numbers of naked boys had climbed up on to the piers of the bridges, where they looked like groups of statuary come to life. Seurat, in this remarkable canvas, has rendered the sultriness of such a day. It throbs with heat.

He was schooled in the Impressionistic tradition, and along with Signac carried their technique to an extreme. *Pointillisme* is the name given to their method of painting in minute and crisply defined strokes of pure prismatic colour. The effect is comparable to that of mosaic, for each touch of the brush left a tiny cube of pigment on the canvas. They did not draw with sweeping strokes, the design of the picture being built up in the way a cross-stitch embroidery proceeds, so that one is always aware of the grid that is its foundation. When this rectilinear sharpness is lost, *pointillisme* was inclined to degenerate into mere stippling. As can be imagined, such a preconceived method of handling brought with it many limitations, and it has not claimed many *dévotes*. Seurat, however, was able to use it with effect.

"La Baignade" is not painted in the strict *pointilliste* manner, though it bears traces of it, notably in the painting of the river and of the grassy bank in the foreground. Any one can see how marvellously he has rendered the heat and light of the scene. Such qualities were indeed the stock-in-trade of the Impressionists, but more remarkable is Seurat's treatment of the figures. Here he has achieved a feeling of volume that reminds one of Piero della Francesca. The youth sitting on the brink is an example of his power of rendering mass. Seurat has sacrificed many things to achieve this. Not one of the figures has his face painted with any attempt at delineation. The trunk and the limbs are what Seurat was interested in. The bank is strewn with torsos; even the discarded clothing seems to be inflated in some mysterious manner. This picture is like a graft of Renoir upon Cézanne.

Seurat died young, and as a result his paintings are comparatively scarce. We are lucky to possess such a fine specimen of his highly individualistic work.

PLATE 98.—LA BAIGNADE : Seurat.

PLATE 99.—PAUL GAUGUIN (1848-1903)
MODERN FRENCH SCHOOL

" FLOWER PIECE "
Tate Gallery

GAUGUIN owes much to Impressionism. We have become so accustomed to the living colour the movement has brought into modern painting, to the doctrine that an artist must think for himself and express his thoughts in his own way, that it is hard to realize what a battle was waged before the new ideas gained acceptance. Gauguin at a very early stage in his career showed that he had an extremely personal way of looking at things. Colour was the quality that attracted him, but to this was joined a very sensitive feeling for pattern. If it was colour, and often highly exotic colour, that stimulated him, it was not colour splashed in " purple patches," any fanfare of trumpets. Colour for him flowed into rhythmic design. So his work has a highly decorative quality. The only charge that can be brought against him is that he is sometimes intoxicated by decoration, stops short at it, and as a consequence in such works lacks a depth of content. That did not, however, happen often. When he went to Tahiti in 1891 he found exactly the environment that suited him. There his work took on a feeling of deep humanity.

Many readers will remember the Gauguins shown in 1932 at the Burlington House Exhibition of French Art. One of these, " Trois Tahitiens," may be cited as revealing his mature genius. A youth, with his beautiful bronzed back turned towards us, is standing between two girls. His gentle averted head is looking to the girl on his left, but one feels that his gaze goes much farther. He seems to carry upon his shoulders all the pathetic submission of the male to those life forces that moulded him, and which hold him in their mesh. So the human content of this picture appears to at least one spectator. Of the solidity of the forms, of the depth of the colour intensities, there can be no dispute.

Gauguin's Tahitian period is not adequately represented in the gallery. This " Flower Piece " shows his superb colouring, but it is hardly representative. Yet how beautiful are the rich purple-blue leaves that balance the composition, and the vermilion flowers seen against the darkness of the vase, sounding their note of sheer joy against the fainter petals and the soft lemon tinge of the background. No one but Gauguin could have painted it.

Gauguin reminds me of Rimbaud. It is possibly a fantastic parallel, but it may suggest a train of thought to one or two readers. Of his importance there can be no question. He is definitely among the greatest colourists who have ever lived.

99

PLATE 99.—FLOWER PIECE: Gauguin.

PLATE 100.—VINCENT VAN GOGH (1853–1890)
MODERN DUTCH SCHOOL

"LANDSCAPE WITH CYPRESS TREES"
Tate Gallery

VAN GOGH'S art and that of Gauguin have much in common. But it is to be found in the spirit of their approach to painting rather than any similarity of result. Van Gogh had a short life, full of suffering, and it was only towards the close of it that he found his real *métier*. He tried many occupations, among them that of an evangelical preacher. It is curious that he did not discover his true bent earlier, for no one could have been more innately a painter than he was. He owed less to schooling than any artist who ever achieved a like distinction.

He had a vivid and passionate apprehension of reality, often, one feels, born of pain—" the notion of some infinitely gentle, infinitely suffering thing." And such was the urge to create, when it came upon him, that he could transfer his vision at white heat on to his canvases. His technique was as intuitive as his inspiration. There is scarcely a painter on record whose method of handling was so spontaneously derived from the impetus in his mind. He worked rapidly in a state of feverish excitement, that ended by consuming him in the fire of his own genius.

He did not go far afield for his subjects. A rush-bottomed kitchen chair, standing on a red-tiled kitchen floor, can, as he sees it, become the text for a marvellous passage of colour, as moving as Turner at his most magical. This "Landscape with Cypress Trees" is full of his flame-like vitality. The cornfield seems to quiver in the breeze and the oppressive heat with the tremor of a mirage. The lambent cypress trees, the hills flowing like lava, and the tortured sultry sky all express the same intensity. And the whole effect is produced in one single consuming moment, as though his hand had never paused until the last rapid sweep of his brush carried his vision to its consummation. It is impossible almost to think of this picture passing through intermediate states of completion.

The Tate Gallery is fortunate in possessing three very beautiful specimens of his work—our landscape, "The Yellow Chair," to which we have referred, and a study of "Sunflowers." Van Gogh's style is so personal that it is impossible to imitate it without becoming merely plagiaristic, and as he held no doctrinaire opinions or theories about art he has not founded a school. The only lesson his pictures teach (if one is minded to press for a lesson over and above so much of delight) is the old Socratic one, "Know thyself." It is the most difficult of all, and the most important.

PRINTED IN GREAT BRITAIN AT THE PRESS OF THE PUBLISHERS

PLATE 100.—LANDSCAPE WITH CYPRESS TREES : Van Gogh.